BADGES

OF HONOR

STORIES OF THE HEAD, HEART, AND HAND

BADGES
OF HONOR
STORIES OF THE HEAD, HEART, AND HAND

COMPILED BY
JOHN M. HINCK, PhD

BookPress® publishing

Published in Des Moines, Iowa, by:

Bookpress Publishing
P.O. Box 71532
Des Moines, IA 50325
www.BookpressPublishing.com

Publisher's Cataloging-in-Publication Data

Names: Hinck, John, editor.
Title: Badges of honor : stories of the head , heart , and hand / compiled by John Hinck, PhD.
Description: Des Moines, IA: Bookpress Publishing, 2021.
Identifiers: LCCN: 2021919288 | ISBN: 978-1-947305-35-9
Subjects: LCSH United States. Air Force--Biography. | United States. Air Force--Military life--Anecdotes. | Leadership. | Conduct of life. | BISAC BIOGRAPHY & AUTOBIOGRAPHY / Military | SELF-HELP / Personal Growth / Success | BUSINESS & ECONOMICS / Leadership
Classification: LCC UG626.2.B26 H56 2021 | DDC 358.4/14/092--dc23

First Edition
Printed in the United States of America
10 9 8 7 6 5 4 3 2 1

CONTENTS

Introduction

Who doesn't like a good story? They can make us laugh, smile, think, cry, and sometimes in a matter of moments. This volume of stories of the head, heart, and hand showcases fourteen selected authors, all leaders in life and teachers in the U.S. Air Force's Leader Development Course. Together, they share *The LDC Way* of leadership with incredible, unique, moving, challenging, and heartfelt stories from life, leadership, and command in the military.

Each author pens an individual chapter that weaves together leadership, character, and values with the personal intersectionality of gender, identity, challenges, and triumphs. While the narratives are diverse and the writing styles are different, each chapter also includes an author biography and leadership lessons to share at the end. This book is built so you can start anywhere and read a chapter at a time or the entire manuscript in an evening. No matter where you open the book, you will be moved to smile, think, laugh, cry, cover your mouth, scream, take notes, nod, and more.

At the end of the book, we offer a few pages so you can

contribute to the work and write a few lines of your own stories. *You are our fourteenth author!*

Enjoy the journey, and as always, thank you for your work!

Go find your story!

Everyone Has a Story

by Martha J. Sasnett

The Weight of Command

I took command of the 42d Force Support Squadron in January 2015. The previous commander was relieved of command, and the squadron had been without a commander for four months. After many conversations with the Group Commander, I understood that I had my work cut out for me. The squadron was demoralized and distrustful of senior leadership. None of the group or wing leadership had explained to the squadron why the commander had been relieved. She was simply there one day and gone the next. The squadron loved this commander, and later I would find out through conversations with squadron members that they felt they had let her down and were the reason for her firing.

Therefore, on the day I took command, I physically felt the weight of my new role. As I looked out among the audience, I knew these Airmen were looking at me with so many questions. Would I be a good commander? Could they trust me? Would I stand up for them? Was I going to care about them? I felt this sense of responsibility and knew that I was going to do everything I could to take care of this squadron and make it successful. One thing I never stopped to reflect on and consider, however, was why this was so important. Taking care of Airmen and their families was always a priority to me as I truly valued service and helping Airmen and their families flourish. I had just never taken the time to examine and reflect on why this was so important to me. I did not know it at the time, but a situation would arise with an Airman that would force me to reflect on my story in order to reconcile what I personally valued against what the Air Force, and my squadron, needed me to value as a commander.

As with any large squadron, there were issues that needed to be dealt with. Fortunately, discipline was not a real problem in my squadron, but we did struggle with physical fitness failures. TSgt Smith was a personnelist in the Commander's Support Staff, and she was a great asset to my admin team. She was a superstar performer who took great care in doing the things I needed before I knew I needed them. Other personnelists on base would seek her advice and her help because she was truly knowledgeable and dependable. She was married with two kids, and her sister lived with her as well. I got to know them well since they visited the squadron regularly. I found out that TSgt Smith was the only one in the family who was working or could drive the one family vehicle. She had a lot of responsibility as the sole provider for the family. This could have contributed to her problem with fitness, though I gave her as much on-duty time as she needed to work out. Even with this, she could not pass her physical fitness test, and by six months into my command, she had failed her test four times within a twenty-four-month period, which is not good. Per Air Force Instruction, this required me to recommend whether or not she be retained in the Air

Force and, based on my decision, possibly some sort of disciplinary action. I had a large range of options, but it was clear from my group leadership that the expectation was the most severe discipline, which was a reduction in rank.

On the surface, it might seem that this decision should have been easy. She didn't meet the standards, and the common punishment was a reduction in rank. I knew that was what my commander expected me to do, but I was very conflicted. In fact, I was more conflicted than I thought I should be, and I did not understand why this was so hard. I am ashamed to admit it, but I didn't fully realize why I struggled with this until years later, when I was attending a course that asked us to reflect on experiences in our past. In the end, I made the decision to reduce TSgt Smith's rank to SSgt, which meant she would have no choice but to leave the Air Force. I didn't realize it at the time, but after much reflection about this situation, I now understand that my personal story that formed my own values was in conflict with those of the organization. I valued families and taking care of Airmen. As a child of divorced parents, with a mother who suffered from substance abuse and mental illness, I spent a lot of time being the adult, always worrying about my two half-sisters. In fact, at one point, they were homeless, living in my mother's car without knowing where their next meal would come from. As I struggled with the decision on TSgt Smith, all I envisioned was sending her family out to the street to be homeless. In my mind, this was not taking care of families. However, the Air Force and the squadron valued accountability, and I had assured the squadron from day one that I would enforce accountability, and I expected them to do the same with me. Without realizing it at the time, I was struggling to reconcile this conflict of values.

I brought TSgt Smith in and told her my decision. She listened, obviously upset about the consequence of being required to separate from the Air Force, especially since she was planning on eventually retiring from the service. She took responsibility for not performing up to the standards and asked me if she could say just one thing. She said, "Thank you." She thanked me for holding her accountable and for following through with what I said I would do. With everything the squadron had been through, she noted, this is exactly what they needed. I was not expecting a reaction like that, but it drove home to me that words may be important, but the actions you take to back up those words (or not) are invaluable. When you tell the squadron something, such as that you will take care of Airmen, it is imperative you think about what that looks like. The squadron will hear you, but they really are watching, so make it count.

Never Judge a Book by Its Cover

While the previous situation ended on a positive note, this was not always the case. I made many mistakes as a commander, and this story is one I think about a lot. I have always felt that I give people the benefit of the doubt before I judge them. Regardless of what I am told about a person, I always try to form my own judgment. I feel that everyone has a story that makes them who they are, and you have to get to know them before you can judge what kind of person they are. However, I am not perfect, and I failed to follow my own advice at a time when I could have possibly had a lifesaving impact on a person.

During my first year of command, my squadron struggled with safety violations. Needless to say, the wing Safety Office was not loved by the leadership in my squadron. The people who had been in the squadron a while made it a point to drop by my office or tell me in meetings about the injustices they were suffering at the hands of our assigned Safety Inspector, TSgt Jones. According to members of my squadron, TSgt Jones was overly gung-ho about safety, and he set out to try to find violations so he could stick it to the squadron. According to them, he obviously had no life, safety was his only interest, and no matter how well they prepared, he would find something wrong during the inspection and would make it seem to me as the commander that the squadron was failing miserably.

Not staying true to my own morals, I took them at their word. At this point, T.Sgt. Jones and I had never sat down and had a conversation. Since we resided on the same floor in our building, we might pass in the hallway and offer a quick hello, but that was the extent of my knowledge of T.Sgt. Jones. October was the month my squadron was due for the annual safety inspection. I had been given a copy of the previous year's report with the warning that T.Sgt. Jones was out to get the squadron. Therefore, when it came time to sit down with T.Sgt. Jones to review his inspection report, it was evident that I had come to the meeting already irritated and on the offensive. I let him give me his input while offering a few curt questions, with the words of my flight leadership echoing in my mind the entire time. He was just an over-the-top, gung-ho safety officer with no life who was trying to find ways in which we were not in compliance. I listened, and when he was finished, I shook his hand and for the most part dismissed him in my mind.

Life in the squadron went on. I tasked the flight chiefs to look at the write-ups, and I continued to see T.Sgt. Jones periodically in our building with only a quick hello and that was it. That is, until January came, and I was forced to see myself in the absolute most shameful way possible. It was right after the new year, in the afternoon on a Sunday, when my phone rang. My group commander was on the line to let me know that we had the death of an active-duty member that I needed to work. As the FSS commander, I was also the mortuary officer for the base, and any active-duty death in our wing would be my responsibility for mortuary and casualty affairs. This was not my first case, so I calmly asked him for additional details and almost hit the floor when he said the name was TSgt Jones from the Safety Office. He had attempted suicide and was currently on life support at a local hospital with little hope for survival. I needed to be ready to proceed once he passed.

All those times I had passed TSgt Jones in the hallway and offered a curt hello washed over me. I thought of the meeting in my conference room where I took no effort to even find out anything about him. Did he have a family? How long had he been at Maxwell Air Force Base? What kinds of things did he like to do? Where was he from originally? All those things that are part of normal conversation to form a connection with someone had never happened. I let other people form my judgment for me, and I never even gave him a chance. Could I have made a difference in his situation? If I had bothered to show that I cared at all, would it have made a difference? I will never know, but the one thing I do know is I will *never* make that mistake again. Everybody has a story, and people are dealing with things we have no idea about every day. Sometimes all it takes is just a little extra effort to make a huge difference. It does not cost a thing, but in the end, it is priceless and could save a life.

Commanders Are Normal People Too

I learned quite a few lessons during my command, and I am grateful for my growth as an officer, leader, and human being as a result of my experiences. Thankfully, there were others who were willing to share their advice and experiences to help lift me up when I needed it. A strong work ethic, diligence, and dedication have always guided my career and the way I conduct myself as an Air Force officer. While those are admirable traits, they can also have negative consequences. It would take fifteen years, assuming my first squadron command, and receiving the shock of a lifetime that would finally help me realize that the way I was leading my people was misguided. I have never been afraid to put in long days and do any job that needs to be done. As a section commander, executive officer, and then commander, I was always the first one in the office and usually the last one to leave. What I didn't realize was the message this was giving my Airmen. In the fall of 2015, approximately six months after assuming command, I found out I was pregnant with my fourth child. My husband and I had no desire to have more children, and we were certainly not expecting this. I immediately went into crisis mode over how this might affect my career. What would the group commander and the wing commander think? I was one of two female commanders in the group and did not want to appear unable to do my job. For about two weeks, I cried regularly over the stress of this situation. What I did not realize at the time was that I was going to learn one of the most valuable lessons of my career from a very unexpected source.

My youngest daughter was taking dance classes, and on a Saturday in December, I was standing with a group of other parents watching a recital. I did not know most of the parents, but I happened to strike up a conversation with a lady standing next to me. The subject of my concern over being a commander and pregnant and what that would look like to everyone else came up. It turns out that this lady was a colonel attending Air War College who had also had a baby while in command. She said, "It was the best thing that could have happened to me and not just because I love my child. It is fantastic that your Airmen can see you being a normal female who can lead but also be a mom. They need to see that it can be done." Her words changed my perspective on the spot because they made so much sense. I had always felt the struggle with work-life balance and the guilt of my family taking time away from my work. I realized in that moment that I owed it to my Airmen, both male and female, to show them this was possible.

The lesson I learned from this very smart colonel continues to guide my career to this day, not just about pregnancy, but about life in general. Obviously, there is a time and a place to share personal details, and I do not share everything about my life, but I want Airmen to know that they can have a career in the Air Force and have a life. Seven months after my son was born, I was diagnosed unexpectedly with cancer. As a squadron commander, people notice when I am out of the office for an extended period of time, so I had to decide what to tell the squadron. Thinking back to the advice from the colonel, I decided to share my journey with them. Situations are not always positive, so I felt that the negative ones were important too. My Airmen may deal with a situation like this or have a family member fall ill, so I wanted them to know that I understood and could be a resource for them.

Being an officer in the Air Force for the last nineteen years has been an honor, and I continue to learn how to be a better officer, leader, and human being every day. I am dedicated to serving my Airmen in the best way possible and never want to stop serving, however I can. I have made many mistakes, and I am sure I will make even more, but I am not too proud to admit that and seek ways to give back to the Airmen who have lifted me up, the Air Force that has given me so much, and this Nation that allows me to be free.

Martha's Leadership Lessons

1. I learned that as a leader, it is okay to allow yourself to be a normal person with life experiences and issues just like everyone else. Let your people see that.

2. Take time for personal reflection. Knowing yourself and understanding your own story are absolutely necessary for good leadership.

3. One of my favorite quotes that speaks to how I try to live my life: *"I've learned that people will forget what you said, people will forget what you did, but people will never forget how you made them feel."*
   –Maya Angelou

MARTHA J. SASNETT

Lt Col Sasnett is a career Force Support Officer in the Air Force with varied leadership experience at the squadron, Air Force Headquarters staff, and Numbered Air Force levels. She has commanded at the Detachment and Squadron levels for a combined total of seven years. Lt Col Sasnett strives to be a servant leader and gets great satisfaction from taking care of people and giving back to the community. Getting to know people and listening to their story, she feels, is the best way to serve them and ensure they have what they need to be successful. She holds a BS in Biology (Western Carolina University), a Master of Arts in Human Relations (University of Oklahoma), and a Master of Strategic Studies (Air University).

Lead with HEART

by Lori R. Hodge

Fish Out of Water

It was November 2017 when I received a phone call from the Air Force Personnel Center. The colonel I spoke with said, "We're considering you for a job. Not just any job. This will be the best job you will ever have! But it will be an incredibly stressful one. This job is located on Guam—a small, beautiful island in the middle of the vast Pacific Ocean. This island has typhoons, tree snakes, giant toads, huge coconut crabs, and your house will come with heaps of gecko poop. This job will require late hours almost every weekday, additional work most weekends, and you will often receive particularly challenging calls in the middle of the night. Furthermore, this job will be outside of your core Public Affairs career field. You will be legally affixed to millions of dollars of government cash and material resources and be directly and personally responsible for hundreds of people—people you'll come to care deeply about. Oh yeah… Screw up, and you'll get fired!"

"All of this, and you're going to tell me this is the best job I'll ever have?!" I replied. But despite all the challenges it presented, I was excited for the opportunity to become a Force Support Squadron (FSS) Commander.

I have always had a deep desire and lasting passion for leading large teams to achieve a unified goal. To this end, when I was presented with the opportunity to lead a big and diverse unit, I jumped at the chance. I did just about everything I could think of to prepare. I attended the FSS Commander's Course and Mortuary Officer's School, read seemingly countless Air Force Instructions (AFIs) and policies, reached out to previous and current commanders for their perspectives and lessons learned, and outlined my command philosophy. I was nervous and was thinking, "What did I just get myself into? What will everyone expect from me? What issues will I be walking into? What if I mess up?" Along with all these intense feelings that typically come with preparing for command, add to it that I was about to command in a completely new career field. As a career Public Affairs Officer, it was clear that initially I would be outside my swim lane. Moreover, the FSS umbrella is enormous. Force Support Squadrons have the widest portfolio and mission sets of any unit in the U.S. Air Force's base/wing structure. Our job in the FSS is to deliver mission support, resiliency, quality of life, and family support capabilities to Airmen and their families. Military and civilian personnel flights, the Airman and Family Readiness program, lodging, childcare, morale, welfare, recreation, education, the post office, dining facilities, and more all fall under the purview of the FSS. The wide range of these organizational responsibilities lends itself to truly diverse squadrons.

Despite the learning curve and huge mission set before me, I knew myself to be a logical, organized, hard-working, and depend-able leader. So while I was nervous, I was confident in my ability to do a good job. I proudly accepted the 36th Force Support Squadron guidon at Andersen Air Force Base, Guam on July 6, 2018. There was no easing into the job. The day after my family and I arrived in Guam, storms were rolling in that quickly formed into a typhoon. Typhoons became one of my major issues, having to deal with four of them while I was in command. While almost everyone else is told to grab essentials for themselves and their families, secure their assets, and hunker down in their homes, FSS is working longer hours preparing the base and protecting facilities by riding out the storm in shelter-in-place locations. Amid the chaos of those first few days, I met with my civilian Deputy, Superintendent, First Sergeant, Operations Officer, and Flight Chiefs to introduce myself, provide my command philosophy, and explain that while I may not be an expert in FSS, I was ready and willing to learn, and that I would be relying on them heavily for their expertise. I told them they would have my unconditional trust.

However, I felt a deep sense that some were skeptical of what I was telling them. I told them we were not going to leave the room until I heard what was on their minds. It was my Superintendent who finally addressed the elephant in the room. He said that he, along with many others in the squadron, were not exactly thrilled at having a non-FSS officer as their commander. He said they were worried I was simply ill-equipped to do a good job. I told him I appreciated his frankness, and I truly did. It was the start of what would be many invaluable blunt and honest dialogues between us. Additionally, I promised him and the others right there and then that I would do them proud. About a week later, I addressed the whole squadron at my first commander's call. I said to that varied group of Airmen that I expected them to show titanic levels of "H.E.A.R.T."—i.e. Honesty, Excellence, Accountability, Respect, and Teamwork—and that I would do the same. These tenets were the cornerstone of my command philosophy. I conveyed these again and again every chance I could. I credit this repetitive sharing, and the subsequent HEART my Airmen showed, for allowing my Airmen to reach out to me during many difficult occasions. There were some tough times. But I trusted my team completely and asked for their help when I needed it. Likewise, through diligence and hard work, I earned their trust and acceptance as well. My command team and I were working beautifully as a team, getting close and making big things happen. Together, we led 400 joint personnel and managed $4 billion in assets that provided rejuvenation, quality of life, and support programming for 39,000 military members, families, and retirees.

Unfortunately, between six and twelve months into my command, my squadron was hit with an unprecedented amount of leadership turnover. My Deputy, Superintendent, First Sergeant, Operations Officer, and three flight commanders all rotated out. This amount of key leadership turnover during this short span of time was potentially damaging. Ironically, it was now my turn to help and educate this new group of squadron leaders and let them lean on me. Like the previous regime, this new command team and I built strong relationships, allowing us to endure and surpass many challenges together.

Accountability

As an officer, we are taught that you are ultimately accountable for your people and mission accomplishment. However, the nuances of this concept when applied to a commander cannot be overstated. In addition to being accountable for your people's performance and careers, you are also accountable for mission success on a much deeper, and often unofficial, personal level. "I promise to give you feedback and hope you will provide me with your honest feedback as well. I ask that you be accountable for your actions. If you make a mistake, own it, correct it, and move on. I, too, will be accountable for my actions, and I ask you to hold me accountable as well." This is what I told my squadron at that first commander's call when discussing accountability in HEART. However, I knew just telling people that you are approachable was not going to work. You must show them, and you have to prove it.

One day during my tenure, one of my senior non-commissioned officers (SNCO) asked if she and one of her Technical Sergeants (TSgt) could meet with me. I knew this TSgt well. We had talked several times in the past. She was a hard charger who volunteered often around the squadron. She was deemed by my command team to be an extremely solid NCO. In fact, she had come to me before, asking me to help push the booster club message. A unit booster club is an unofficial organization that conducts fundraisers to collect money for unit functions, e.g., the squadron holiday party.

As the meeting started, I could see they were clearly uncomfortable. I asked them what I could do for them, and they both just stared at each other. After an awkward silence, the SNCO said that the NCO had something she would like to bring to my attention. The TSgt started slowly, "Well, ma'am, you said you want honest feedback, and I wanted to let you know that I don't feel we're getting the support we need for the booster club."

I knew that we were struggling to get volunteers and had low turnout at meetings.

As she continued, I quickly realized she was not talking about squadron member support; she was talking about support from me, her commander! She said that I had been immensely helpful in encouraging volunteers for the booster club. However, she and the other Airmen never saw me at the meetings or fundraising events. It hurt to hear those words. I sat there in silence for a few moments as

I processed this. I was asking my squadron members to do something I was not even doing myself. I could see she was worried that perhaps she had gone too far or had said too much. I quickly put her at ease by telling her that she was right, that I needed to walk the walk. I thanked her for her candor, then asked her to brief me on future events so I could ensure I was there.

Who knows how many other Airmen were thinking the same thing? There I was, asking them to volunteer during their off-duty time while I myself had not been fully invested. I was of course incredibly busy, but regardless, this thought had not even crossed my mind. I had a commander's call about a month after this meeting. As I was preparing my remarks, I asked the TSgt if she was okay with me bringing up our conversation. I told my squadron I'd ask them for their feedback from day one, and I was happy to say someone had done just that. She had held me accountable, and I wanted my team to know and encourage more people to do the same thing. This would not be the last time that I, and subsequently my squadron, would benefit from someone reaching out to me with invaluable information.

My Difficult Conversation

It was raining hard that night, when I received what seemed at first to be a quite common message on my work phone. The message was from one of my NCOs asking if she could talk to me. It had been another long, *helluva* day, in another long, *helluva* week at Andersen Air Force Base. We were in the throes of the base's COVID-19 crisis response, and my squadron was fully engaged in a slew of personnel accountability, lodging, and facilities issues. I expected she wanted to talk about something related to this ongoing crisis, but I was mistaken. As we started talking, she immediately began crying. She started crying so hard it was difficult to understand her. I assumed someone close to her had passed away. As she calmed down, she described why she was so upset. I realized she was talking about someone who had died, but this was not someone she knew. What she described was horrific! But I did not fully understand why the news was hitting her so hard. I was clearly missing something. We ended the call with her thanking me for listening, and just before hanging up she gave me a charge. She said, "Ma'am, I think it would be powerful if the squadron could hear from you about this."

I had not been paying attention to the news that day or frankly that whole week. I was consumed with COVID-related actions. Once we hung up, I quickly went to the internet and watched the video. That phone call was one day after George Floyd died. Straight away, I consulted with my Superintendent and First Sergeant to come up with ideas on our proposed way ahead. I was asking myself and them, "What should I do? Send an email, have a commander's call, or meet with Airmen one-on-one?" At the time, we were unsure whether immediate engagement was the right move. Base leadership had not said anything yet, and I did not want to get ahead of my chain of command. At that time, most of the Air Force had been silent on this incident, and my speaking out on such a sensitive matter frankly scared the hell out of me. As you know, things heated up drastically over the next few hours and days, and this quickly developed into a colossal international story with unprecedented repercussions for our nation. Racism in all its forms is inexcusable, and clearly this was an unspeakable act. This was an indescribably sensitive issue, and my best intentions aside, by speaking out, I could end up doing more harm than good.

My internal struggle was that I had been brought up in a world where the sentiment was, I, as a white person, was not supposed to talk about "these kinds of things." Reaching out to Airmen was the right thing to do and in concert with the values I had incorporated into my unit. However, in addition to not knowing how my efforts would be received, I did not know at the time what the larger Air Force's reaction would be, or if there was a deemed lack of one, and how that would play out. However, my NCO was right. It was clear my Airmen needed me to do something… to say something at the very least.

Knowing that in critical situations, base leadership preferred commanders to make decisions and act versus ask for permission, I moved out before anyone in my chain of command. First, I sent an email to my entire squadron with my thoughts addressing the horrible incident. I met with my Flight Commanders and SNCOs to have a candid discussion. They shared their raw feelings and their relatable experiences and perspectives of what was happening in the world and gave some indication of how others in the squadron were feeling as well.

Over the next two days, we set up several small group meetings with Airmen to have frank conversations and to allow them to share their perspectives. I told them I, like them, was deeply disturbed by the death of George Floyd. I said that these were very disturbing times for all of us, and that these issues were often too emotional to even talk about, but that we must talk. I said then, as I do today, that we must reaffirm our commitment not to discriminate against anyone based on race, color, gender, national origin, religion, or sexual orientation. I told my Airmen I hoped they had established relationships and formed bonds that allowed them to speak candidly with families, friends, peers, supervisors, and leaders.

Fortunately, I believe our squadron had already forged such a values-based culture. That NCO felt empowered to reach out to me directly because we had established a foundation of trust from the beginning that encouraged Airmen to speak. We had HEART.

Without that NCO messaging me, my actions would have been delayed and far less impactful. Sometimes, the right voice comes at the right time from someone other than a senior leader. She felt confident that I could make a positive impact on the squadron. Really, I was simply amplifying her voice. I thanked that exemplary NCO for having the courage to send me that simple yet so significant message that rainy night and for feeling so strongly that my speaking out right away would be helpful to our teammates. She opened a pathway for us to have some very meaningful and challenging conversations.

That Colonel from AFPC was right! Despite the challenges, and many times precisely because of them, leading as a squadron commander, part of a team I was directly and personally responsible for and cared deeply about, was the best job I have ever had.

Lori's Leadership Lessons

1. Lead with authenticity. Don't try to be someone you're not. People will see through it. Embrace and fortify the strengths you bring to the table while also forging honest relationships that genuinely value input from your team.

2. Create a culture of open and frank two-way communication from the outset. Treat everyone with respect but be accountable to one another and yourself. Walk the walk.

3. Don't shy away from vulnerability. When teams see leaders acknowledging and working through their vulnerabilities toward a shared purpose, it creates trust.

LORI R. HODGE

Lt Col Hodge is a prior-enlisted Texas native and a 2002 graduate from Air Force ROTC at Angelo State University. She is a former Force Support Squadron (FSS) Commander and career Public Affairs Officer (PAO). She has held a variety of positions at the Wing, Major Command, and Air Staff levels, and in Joint and Coalition environments. Lt Col Hodge has deployed to Guyana, South America; Baghdad, Iraq; and Kabul, Afghanistan. She was awarded the Bronze Star for her public affairs actions in Afghanistan and is among a few PAOs to be selected as FSS Commanders. Lt Col Hodge practices authentic leadership. Her experiences have taught her that personifying and embodying the same values and behaviors that one expects from their team is the most effective form of leadership. She has a Master of Arts in Strategic Communication.

You Can't Lead Just a Little

by Mary Carnduff, MD

Good leaders guide their teams to do what's right because they understand the "why." Good commanders create a culture in which their teams feel supported, respected, and empowered, and those teams do what's right because their integrity allows nothing less.

You Care or You Don't; the Rest is Just Detail

When I took the guidon that signified my assumption of command, I had a million things I wanted to accomplish. But in command, competing priorities compelled me to decide what my squadron needed and focus our energy accordingly. I quickly realized that I approached these decisions through the lens of my personal values, so I had to balance what I believed with what the mission required.

My values are rooted in my faith. I'm comfortable discussing religion and most other topics, so most who know me are aware of my opinions. But like most people, there's more to me than the boxes

I check. I believe in equality for everyone regardless of the qualities that make us unique. I believe in respectful dissent—even when we disagree, we must get along. I believe the Dallas Cowboys are America's team and Michael Jordan is the greatest basketball player of all time. But as a young officer, I didn't value family. My focus has always been the mission—I care that my team is healthy and effective, but I didn't particularly care about their lives outside of work. I didn't try to remember spouses' names or what grades their kids were in. This sentiment wasn't an accident. My relationship with my own family had been complicated for a good portion of my life. I had lived through a not-so-great marriage, and cancer took my ability to have children when I was 33 years old. Consciously or unconsciously, these experiences negatively impacted my view of "family." Imagine my frustration at promotions or awards when someone would tell me, "Oh, you wouldn't be here without the support of your family." I thought, "Like hell, I wouldn't! I'm here despite that mess." Going into command, however, I wanted to ensure my values aligned with those in my charge. I had no problem with Airmen knowing how I felt about issues, but I also wanted them to feel welcome to approach me on any topic, knowing I would listen without judgment. I wanted them to know I cared about not just the mission, but them as people.

To build rapport, I created opportunities to get to know my Airmen. One such effort was to deliver good and bad news in person. As a result, the first time I met one of my Airmen, it was to tell her she had not been selected for promotion. Despite having just moved into the squadron, she took the disappointing news in stride. In that discussion, and in several after, we talked about the ways she could make a positive impact in her section. It wasn't always smooth. As they consolidated into a team, we also discussed leading with empathy, and how to encourage her people rather than steamrolling over them. She was eager to learn and remained dedicated to the team's success, so I was proud to see her progress.

I do my best thinking in the afternoon, so I stayed late most days. Knowing this, it was common for members to swing by as the day ended and stay if they needed to chat. One day, she came into my office on the verge of tears and sat down. After a moment, she explained that regarding her pregnancy, which she'd recently shared with me, she'd received some terrible news. Ultrasound showed possible abnormalities in her baby that could lead to serious disabilities, that is if it survived to term. Her mother's response had been to recommend an abortion. She said she'd come to my office because she knew that I cared about her. So we cried together for a moment. Then we talked about the medicine. The great thing about being a doctor in these situations is that it's easier to go back to the facts. We talked about the range of issues and severity, and what that might mean for her family.

Then she asked me what I would do… and what she should do. It should have been simple for me to answer; logic says my religion, history, and values dictate a clear choice. However, logic isn't the overriding factor in many life-changing decisions. And again, there's more to me than the categories in which I fit. As a woman, I feel this is a personal decision. As a doctor, I know the toll chronic illness can take on a family, especially when that illness occurs in a child. This moment shook me to the core. I was furious at her mom for hurting her, and it reminded me of the pain I had tried to forget. I was frustrated that life might deal her such a terrible hand after giving her hope, much as I had felt in the unnumerable times I'd thought I had things figured out. And I was worried pain would cloud my judgment. I didn't want to push her to a decision she'd regret. So after thinking for a few minutes that felt like hours, I told her that if I was in her position, I would do what my heart said was right, and so should she. And I told her that no matter what she decided, I would support her 100 percent and we would use every resource the Air Force had to offer. Then I asked what she wanted. She wanted to love her baby and give him a chance, so that's what we were going to do. She continued to check in and continued to do rockstar work because that's what rock stars do. There were a few bumps along the way, but we kept praying for a little more time. A few weeks before she was due, she started having contractions. She was admitted to the hospital and placed on bedrest. When I visited her, she was scared, but comforted by the overwhelming support of the squadron.

Then the baby was born, and that beautiful little man came into this world absolutely perfect. She recovered quickly, and a few months later, when she was back at work, our world came full-circle when I got to tell her that she'd earned that next stripe.

Leading by Example is Not Enough

My squadron was filled with outstanding performers, but when I arrived, I encountered a widespread perception of unfairness in awards and opportunities. Many Airmen felt that recognition was based on opaque and arbitrary systems rooted in favoritism. To address this concern, we began several processes to increase trans-parency and endeavored to ensure that the processes were easily understood by everyone. One such effort was a decoration review worksheet. For a decoration to be considered, the flights would complete an evaluation which recommended for or against the medal, with rationale and suggestions for improvement if necessary. The comments were reviewed by the leadership chain and signed by the member. If I needed clarification, I engaged with the supervisor and flight leadership to better understand their rationale. This technique empowered the supervisors and turned them into stronger advocates for their Airmen.

Halfway through my command, one of my young Company Grade Officers (CGO) submitted a recommendation for a decoration for one of his Airmen. The officer was very engaged and strongly supported the Airman he'd been supervising, but the assessment was a surprise given the Airman's most recent performance report. I asked for more information and the Flight Commander, Flight Chief, and supervisor came together to discuss the recommendation.

The young officer presented an argument supporting the member's attitude and cooperation with him over the last several months. However, the flight leaders had perspective on the member's entire tour of duty—they reported the member had been removed from a special duty, and upon return to the flight had missed significant work due to legal and medical appointments. The member had been absent rather than present for the better part of a year, and as a result had neither managed programs nor supervised others in a rank-appropriate manner. The leaders discussed the situation at length and reached a consensus, submitting the decoration worksheet with a recommendation for no medal. I concurred, and the matter was closed.

Another touchpoint I maintained was an exit interview with every squadron member. When we met, the Airman was irritated and uncooperative. After several one-word responses, I asked whether the decoration was the source of frustration. The Airman explained that the Air Force owed everyone a decoration because if the service cares about the "whole Airman," then everyone should get an award no matter what, and the flight should have been more supportive. I disagreed and explained the criteria I used, that I expected sustained superior performance in rank-appropriate duties. We discussed the member's performance, but the Airman was insistent that the decoration was a right I had unfairly denied.

I was committed to finding common ground with the Airman, so I asked, "Do you feel that you did an entire tour of work for the Air Force?"

The Airman answered, "No."

I said, "Well, when you were here, do you feel that you did outstanding work?"

"Not really."

"Do you feel like the work you did was appropriate to your rank and time in service?"

"No."

This Airman was the same rank as the acting Flight Chief. I asked, "Do you feel you are doing the same caliber of work as your Flight Chief?"

"Well, no."

"But you think you deserve the same decoration for doing a fraction of the work?"

Adamantly, "Yes."

Nonplussed, I confessed that given the Airman's perspective, I did not think I'd be able to find an answer that would satisfy them. The interview concluded shortly afterward, and the member left the base as scheduled.

Two months later, I was called into my boss's office to address an Inspector General complaint alleging I was a racist. The complaint stated I gave decorations to white people, but not Black people. Specifically referenced was a white Airman who had received a decoration and a Black Airman who had been denied. Per our established protocol, the flights had advocated for the first Airman, and I had concurred. You just read the story of the second.

The complaint took me aback. My boss asked me to respond, and I realized I had no idea what the demographics of my awards were. I pulled in my First Sergeant and the Flight Chief and told them about the situation. They listened, frustrated by the complaint because they, too, had been committed to creating fair processes. We went over our procedures, pulled all our documentation, and reviewed our discipline and awards through a new lens.

After a discussion of the best way forward, we addressed the complaint. Fortunately, the processes to create transparency and consistency were effective and tangible. The evaluation sheets and awards statistics showed no trends toward bias of any kind and had clear feedback and rationale. The information was compiled, and after review by my boss and the Inspector General, the complaint was closed.

Mary's Leadership Lessons

1. Although my values helped me to create a framework of trust with my Airmen, setting the example was not enough. A leader must send a clear message. I used to say all my Airmen are blue, but it's not that I don't see color; I just don't see it as a positive or negative attribute. It is a factor, however, because our culture influences how we behave and how we are received by others, but my assessment of the role of bias was mostly internal. I was aware of bias in disagreements or discipline. I was aware of bias because when we formed teams, I liked cultural and cognitive diversity to foster creativity. I was aware of bias because I am personally comfortable with race and culture and how they mix. But my awareness fell short. It's not enough to be for or against anything you want to inculcate into your squadron. If you make your Airmen guess what you believe, you introduce the risk that they will guess wrong. You must be vocal, transparent, and tireless to create the culture your Airmen deserve.

2. Consistency in action is powerful. My efforts to connect with my Airmen established a baseline for what they could expect from me. When my Airman had an earth-shattering problem to deal with, she wasn't worried about my judgment because she knew that I cared. When my character was attacked, I had several advocates ready to defend my integrity. Values must be accompanied by words and action. Culture is not an accident. If we want to instill behaviors and beliefs in those we lead, we can't do it by force or fear; we must use every day to create an environment in which the alternatives are unacceptable, trust is earned and reciprocated, and every Airman is invested in the squadron's success.

3. In many circumstances, our values feel compromised when we try to support people who might make choices we would not. But this mindset misses the fact that our experiences, our family dynamics, and our understanding of "basic principles" are unique. How we even define these words can be vastly different, but their ubiquity lulls us into a sense of complacency. Regardless of our frame of reference, the choice is binary: you care about Airmen, or you don't. I do, so I will always try to find a way to support them knowing I don't have to compromise who I am or what I believe. This can be a challenge when we support someone with whom we disagree, but everything I hold dear tells me the effort is worth it.

MARY CARNDUFF, MD

Lt Col Carnduff originally planned to serve four years as an orthopedic surgeon and separate from the Air Force. After three duty stations and two deployments, she found herself both frustrated and inspired to apply for command. In previous units, she had discovered the influence of good leaders was indisputably present, but the impact of bad leaders was also profound. Lt Col Carnduff makes mistakes and still has much to learn about leadership, but she commanded the way she has learned to live her life: full-speed, all-in, and trying to do the right thing every time. Lt Col Carnduff is a board-certified orthopedic surgeon and fully mission qualified flight physician; she has earned Masters Degrees in Business Administration and Strategic Studies, certification as a Physician Executive, and is a Fellow of the American Academy of Orthopaedic Surgeons.

Generational Leadership Lessons

by Stephanie Q. Wilson, PsyD

Mantras of Character

When I think about leadership and the lessons I have learned, I must go first to my parents. I come from a family of educators, nurses, and military members. Both of my parents were officers, something not normally seen in African American households, then or now. We were usually the sole family on base with this make-up, and my parents taught me that it was not the skin that mattered but what my mind and spirit brought to the table. They also taught me to look at others in the same way.

My parents led through faith and humility. My dad always told me that if you become the best at what you do, no one can deny you access to the room because they would look like a fool not to hire the best… and no one enjoys looking like a fool. My mother taught me to lead with compassion and to always remember to train my successor. Someone who is invaluable in any position will likely remain in that position and could be prevented from growth or upward movement, and I wanted to grow. These are the core leadership lessons I left home with when I began my military career. Have faith things will turn out the way they are meant to, have humility while becoming the best at what you do, and lead with compassion while training your successor.

These mantras shaped my character, how I value what others bring to the table, and how I have seen myself. I know others were not raised the same, but I know that even if the words we said were different, the foundational concepts of humanness and compassion would override any lexical disagreement. It is interesting how these lessons have manifested throughout my military career in ways both big and small.

My Journey

I commissioned into the military from the Reserve Officer Training Corps (ROTC) and as such was told that if I flew to my first base, the military would pay for that and a rental car. Having just acquired my first vehicle on my own, the opportunity to drive from North Carolina to California was exciting and scary. In this instance, the service reimburses you for your travel after your arrival. No one ever briefed us on advances or how to get money to begin the trip. At least no one ever briefed me.

So as I plotted my trip, planned my stops, and took stock of my bank account and expected costs, I was confident I could make it with money to spare. I would be getting paid from the day of entry, and since I was headed to a training base first, then my base of record, I would have a few months before deposits and other household setup expenses would be required. I was also lucky to have a generous family who celebrated my graduation and commissioning with the best gift a young person could get—money. Cash to start my new life and the means to get to where I wanted to go to start my career was a gift in itself… and I thought I was ready.

A college friend of mine was ready to be my road partner. We were going to take a girls' trip and head out on the open road. I was excited to share this experience with a friend and someone I knew I really got along with and could share both the silence and the loudness of a road trip. We differed enough to be interesting but were similar enough that we did not have conflicts. But two weeks before we were scheduled to leave, my friend called me with some news. An internship she had applied for but was told she did not get had called her back. The candidate they had selected had chosen to do something else, and they wanted to know if she was still free. The internship started the week we were supposed to be driving, and she was pumped to take on this challenge that would set her on her career path. I was so excited for her, and also pumped about driving cross-country by myself, but my parents vetoed that idea quickly.

From two different households, love and care showed up in the form of "nope, nope, nope!" My dad was not excited about the prospect, and my mom was even more against it. Due to the timing, neither of them could come with me, either, but my boyfriend (who later would become my husband) said he had time off and could make the trip with me if a few of our travel days could be arranged over a weekend.

My parents were also not pleased with this idea, but I was an adult with a job, so my boyfriend, James, became my road partner. The trip was amazing, and we learned a lot about each other. I also learned the power of having someone who believes in you and supports your career choices, even the ones inconvenient to them. He helps to make me better by also believing things happen in the way they are meant to be and that everything can help you grow as a person, and how fun it was to be on that journey with someone who cared about the outcome!

This lesson has been a foundation for me in leadership. Everyone's journey is their own, and my role is to help make it easier if I can, but also to hold each person responsible for their choices because that is how we help each other grow. This also reinforced the first leadership lesson I learned as a child—that things will always work out the way they are meant to.

Unlike my departure from home, leaving my training base was neither smooth nor easy. I reached out to the sponsor who was supposed to guide me through the process, but never really got much information. There were issues with my pay at the training base, and they said they could not fix the problems until I had arrived at my home base, but as I looked at my account and considered my trip, I started to get concerned. Everyone kept telling me things would be fine, so I believed them.

After my drive from California to my host base in Montana, I was pumped about officially getting started. I had not chosen this career field, and I honestly felt like I had no idea what I was walking into. I was nervous and scared, but I was also extremely excited about my new life.

As I approached the front gate, the guard peered into my car, took my ID, and said, "Oh, ma'am, we don't get many of you here!"

"Okay," I replied, "Well, um, can you tell me how to get to lodging?" I followed his directions and got to base lodging, but as I walked in, the young woman behind the desk called out, "We do not have room for you here!"

I stopped in the middle of the welcome area and noted the irony of feeling unwelcome there. Then I saw her open the computer and say, "We are under renovation, and we have no rooms."

PHEW! I thought. I was already on edge after driving twelve hours that day on mountain pass roads and missing my best friend's wedding just to make it to my base, so I reminded myself not to let my bad day be hers by being mean to her.

She helped me get a letter allowing me to stay off-base, but this would be much more expensive than my budget. She showed me the map to get to my hotel downtown, and as I was leaving, she looked at me and said, "You won't like it here. They do not like US here." And she slid her brown finger across her brown hand, the universal sign for black folks among other black folks.

I drove to the hotel, called my sponsor, and told her I was in town. She said she was too busy to meet with me but would see me Monday in the building. It was Saturday afternoon. I was in a town, a state, a place I had never been, in a hotel, alone.

"Sure. See you Monday," I replied, thinking I guess this is how we treat everyone. I guess this is how we welcome people.

That night, I sat in the lobby of the hotel and ate my dinner at the bar reading a book. The next day, I drove around town, which took all of thirty minutes, and went back to my hotel room and sat alone trying to figure out how to be my best in a place that did not seem to offer me the same. The only way I knew to become my best was to just do it. I would not let the cold welcome I had received be my final judgement on the location or my abilities. So I just jumped into work!

I did not understand a lot, but I admitted it and asked questions. I followed my Senior Non-Commissioned Officer (SNCO) around to all the meetings until I figured out what was happening. I read everything I could get my hands on and went to help the people I had the honor of leading whenever I could. I did a lot of things wrong, but I must have gotten some things right because instead of me chasing people down to get help, people started seeking it from me. I fell in love with helping people months before I had fallen in love with the mission I supported.

When I asked about how to get people awarded, my supervisor said only, "Oh, are you chasing that?" He never answered my questions on how quarterly, annual, or any other awards worked.

But my SNCO did, and he had overheard my question. He pulled me aside and said, "I got you, ma'am." He taught me maintenance, safe practices, and what should make my hair stand on end. He pushed me to speak up more in meetings and took my suggestions seriously. He chuckled when I put Glade Plug-ins around the office because I said, "sometimes folks' thoughts are smelly." He told me I was the first female in the shop in over a decade, and he was happy it was me. He helped me learn about winter weather in Montana and laughed at how many clothes I would have on when I came in and when I discovered the plugs in the parking lot were not for Christmas lights but block heaters so fluids in your vehicle don't freeze while you are at work.

I came in and tried to do my best every single day. My best was to work a sound maintenance schedule that took care of the mission but also the other needs of my Airmen, from appointments to family obligations. I also had to learn to budget for a section and how to tell people they were wrong and celebrate wins when they were right.

This, to me, was the reward, and I did not think I was really noticed until it was time to rotate jobs and I got a great one. This new job had another SNCO who taught me how to help people through grief, suicide attempts, and the loss of a child and even how to lead people I did not like. In this new role, I began to get awards, but I felt odd because I did not think it was my work, but that of my team, that deserved recognition.

My new supervisor, who was amazing, told me this is how it works. If we, as leaders, maintained an environment in which people could do well, then we were doing our part for the team. Though it still feels odd to this day, I learned to use this and work hard to recognize leaders who built the right environment and set the right tone for the team. I dug into writing awards for teams and recognizing people in small and big ways.

I fully believe this philosophy has saved me from becoming bitter over other people's bad days and has protected my good days from being impacted. My job is to set the climate for the team. To make sure I know enough to help push the right ideas and safe practices forward for the betterment of our Air Force family and for our mission. I am a fan of recognition, but I really love the notes from people I have had the honor of helping in the past or seeing a workplace continue to thrive after I depart. I feel as if my spirit is fed, and I feel part of a team when I see the team succeeding through a healthy culture.

I learned that having humility in working to be the best does not mean you cannot be proud of your accomplishments or those of the people around you. Humility is a reminder that not everything revolves around you. It is the history of you and all the things you have failed and succeeded in doing as well as the team that has helped you. Becoming the best in your field does not mean you have to step on or belittle others. As my dad said, "If you become the best, people will hire you because no one wants to be the fool who missed the opportunity to hire the best." I am so proud to have been a part of great teams who helped me bring my best to the table. My parents are two for three so far in these leadership lessons.

Leading with compassion while training your successor took me a little while to understand. Some people believe being compassionate means not holding people accountable. It is easy to mix compassion with wanting to be liked, and I did that for a while. I also learned that my job as a leader is to maintain standards and ensure parity, not necessarily equity, in my decisions. Failing to do so will lead to conflict because what I might do for one person will not look the exact same as what I have done for another, leaving people upset.

The discussion about parity versus equity is important in my home as it also helps to train my successors. It helps to establish family boundaries that I hope will be maintained as the kids grow up and establish homes of their own. This mantra of leading with compassion while training your successor has also shown up time and time again at work. People need to know that they are not a cog in the machine, simply to be thrown away if something goes "wrong," and those I train should not have to re-learn lessons I myself have already fought through.

One example of this was an individual who committed the crime of smoking marijuana, which is illegal for military personnel. The person later admitted to the action and took the punishment of removal from the military with an "other than honorable" discharge. As a leadership team, we made sure they had the appropriate time to process out of the service and gain employment in the community so that we were not sending them back to the civilian world without some type of anchor. Our team even made sure they knew some folks who had settled in the same area they were looking to settle, so if they needed an ear, they had it.

On the day I was scheduled to present the official separation paperwork to the Airman, I noticed they were emotional. Their face was red, as if they had been crying, and they were fidgeting more than normal outside my office. I went over to my First Sergeant (or "shirt," in military parlance) and asked if they could talk to the Airmen one more time before we presented paperwork and see what could be wrong aside from the obvious issue of being discharged. My shirt came back into my office ten minutes later and quickly shut the door. He stated the Airman's spouse had just lost their father about two weeks ago, and when the spouse had gone to the funeral, having received permission from their civilian manager to miss three shifts to attend to their family, a new manager had come in and said he hadn't approved the missed shifts, so the spouse had gotten fired that morning. With the Airman separating that day, and the holiday weekend coming up, it looked like it would take another pay period to get the entire matter straight, and during that time, no money would be coming into the household.

I asked my shirt to call legal and see if we could delay presentation of the separation paperwork until after the holiday weekend, which crossed over another pay period. This would allow the Airman to receive a week's worth of pay and benefits, which would get them to the first paycheck in their new job. It would not be an quitable trade, but it would at least not bankrupt them during that time. Our team was able to get the determination that it was fine and reschedule appointments within twenty minutes. I was so impressed.

So at the time I was supposed to be handing over paperwork, I called the Airman in and told them what was going to happen. I informed them they would not be separating that day but on the following Tuesday and why. I also let them know that it was their record before the crises that helped make this decision easy for me, but that it was also the right and compassionate one.

The following Tuesday, the Airman came in, and we presented their paperwork. Last I heard, the Airman and was doing fine in their new job, as was their family, and the spouse was able to find work somewhere else and was happier at that job than at the previous one.

None of the decisions or actions I had taken were completed in a vacuum. The leadership team that oversaw the Airman watched and learned how to lead with compassion while holding individuals accountable for their actions. The outcome was that we were going to separate an Airman, and that was done. We did not need to make it even worse for the Airman if we could help it. I knew this team "got it," and that I had done well in training my successors, when another situation about timing someone's departure from our service came up and they provided viable solutions that benefitted the organization and the Airman. In fact, the only reason they even needed me to be aware was due to coordination with another commander, otherwise they were empowered to make those calls on their own, and they did it! They led with compassion, and the team was better for it. Work like this continues to feed my spirit and make me a better and more authentic leader because of it.

Sometimes we forget our humanity in the midst of decision-making. Leading with compassion helps us to remember this, and training our successor helps allow us to move up the chain of leadership building others up who remember lessons previously learned.

There are so many leadership books and guides and stories one can pull from. I love reading them and seeing what I can glean from them to add to my toolbox for self-improvement. Yet no matter what I read, I still return to the lessons my parents taught me: have faith things will turn out the way they are meant to, have humility while becoming the best at what you do, and lead with compassion while training your successor. Lead well…

Stephanie's Leadership Lessons

1. Find an answer to the question, "How are you and those you lead fed?"

2. Become the best with humility.

3. Lead with compassion.

STEPHANIE Q. WILSON, PsyD

Stephanie Q. Wilson is a wife, a mother of four, a military officer (Colonel), a scholar, and a friend. She has held the honor of command at the squadron level twice, first as the 90th Munitions Squadron Commander and second as the 90th Missile Maintenance Squadron Commander, both at Francis E. Warren AFB, Wyoming. Stephanie completed her bachelor's degree at Clemson University and went on to complete her doctorate in psychology while simultaneously deploying, completing military professional education, adding to her family, and moving three times. She believes you can learn leadership lessons from anyone and from anywhere and that you should give yourself grace as you determine how to integrate those lessons into your personal leadership style.

Guardian Angel, the Rule, and Clarity of Purpose

by Matthew A. "Astro" Astroth

Guardian Angel

It's a frosty morning. Beep, beep, beep, beep, smack! The time is 0400 local. Time to get up. I can hear a similar routine around the other five rooms inside our 18' x 36' uninsulated plywood living structure. Normally, this is the time the crew gets up to hit the gym, but today is special. We have been tasked with forward deploying our AC-130U Spooky gunship south to Kandahar Air Base to support the kickoff of Operation Moshtarak in the Helmand Province of Afghanistan. As I reach to turn off my electric blanket, I consider the perfect timing for the change in scenery. We had arrived in country at the end of January and had been operating out of snow-covered Bagräm Air Base for about a month. Instead of waking up to freezing temperatures, the climate around Kandahar would be much warmer with the combination of lower elevation and southern latitude. This thought alone boosts my morale as I slide my toes into my frozen boots.

The crew was also excited for the increased opportunity to engage the enemy since these types of operations usually require an increased need for aerial artillery support. Up to this point, our trip had been fairly quiet. In June 2009, President Obama had assigned General Stanley McChrystal as the commander of U.S. and coalition forces in Afghanistan. By February 2010, the "hearts and minds" campaign was in full swing, which included a significant decrease in nighttime raids against the Taliban and their associated terrorist network. The crew was ready to put their training and honed combat skills into action.

A couple of days later, we found ourselves sitting in the doublewide trailer that served as our makeshift crew briefing room. Our intelligence analyst duct taped a white bed sheet to the wall and used a projector to provide us an overview of Operation Moshtarak. We were in theater to support approximately 4,000 U.S. Marines tasked to clear approximately 2,000 Taliban fighters from their largest stronghold in Helmand Province. This operation was the beginning of what would be the largest joint operation up to that point in the Afghanistan War. For scale, the city of Marjah is 100 square miles, roughly the equivalent of Amarillo, Texas. During the briefing, we were provided the latest imagery of friendly force positions, known enemy locations, and the current operating picture. The marines had been engaged in heavy fighting as they slowly advanced from block to block across the city. My crew was eager to assist. With callsigns, coordinates, and frequencies in hand, we stepped to the aircraft to jump into the fight.

The sun was setting on the horizon as we performed our preflight checklists. For this operation, fast movers like F-16s and F-15Es would cover the twelve-hour daylight window, and we were tasked to cover the twelve-hour period of darkness. The distinct drone of the AC-130's four propellers as it orbits the battlefield at night, combined with its overwhelming lethal firepower, are known to strike fear into the hearts of the enemy. This nighttime terror largely influences the AC-130's nickname among Taliban fighters as the "Spitting Witch" or "Angel of Death." The reputation of looming death was a large part of the reason our deployment had been so slow. Every time we arrived overhead to support an operation, the target objective immediately surrendered as soon as the whirl of our propellers was audible. Little did I know, I was about to gain a better appreciation of the effects of that reputation.

Shortly after we arrived at the aircraft, the propellers were spinning, and we taxied to the runway. Our sortie profile included takeoff, a weapons system check over the range south of base, and twelve hours of on-call, close air support to include air refueling before returning to base. Marjah is only 100 nautical miles west of Kandahar Air Base, so it was only a quick thirty-minute flight to arrive above the embattled city. Once cleared inside the restricted operating zone by the air traffic controller, we checked in with the fire support officer. He thanked us for the support and directed us to check in with Charlie Company due to the significant amount of enemy contact they had seen throughout the day. Eager to help, we dialed up the frequency and immediately listened to a request I will never forget.

Upon check-in, we were greeted by the unmistakable voice of a marine joint terminal air controller who had been receiving and returning small arms fire all day. We provided our standard ordinance profile, time available until air refueling, and sensor tasking. He replied with the most humbling radio call: "41, 52, I'm sorry, but we don't have any work for you right now. We've been under constant small arms fire all day, but when you showed up, they all went home. They fear you being overhead. If you don't mind, could you simply scan the area and provide security while we get some sleep? We haven't slept in three days."

We replied, "Copy all, and absolutely no problem. You get some rest. No one will mess with you while we are here." For the next twelve hours, my crew maintained precision focus over the battlefield. This night, we were not the "Angel of Death," but the Guardian Angel over every Marine in Marjah. To this day, I am still proud of that crew's demonstration of maturity and professionalism as we provided overwatch.

Too often, the wrong message is glorified from combat stories. Hollywood prefers to sensationalize the hero who lays waste to the enemy in a hail of bullets and explosions. In contrast, sometimes the most rewarding combat experience comes from the night we keep our weapons cold.

The Rule

"Pilot, I've got a problem." This phrase was the theme for today. It was summer of 2010 in Iraq, and my AC-130U gunship crew was having one of those nights where nothing seemed to work. The power was out in the alert facility, so pre-launch duties were a chore. Fortunately, our intelligence officer saved the day by finding a work-around to get us the products we needed for mission execution. During preflight checks, the flight engineer had found a few maintenance problems with the aircraft, but I could always count on him to get them fixed in a hurry. Once airborne, I heard the lead gun over the intercom: "Pilot, there is a problem with Gun 3." That was the 105mm Howitzer. "We need to take it offline to fix it." I responded, "Thanks, guns. Let me know when it's fixed." Despite all the problems, I knew this crew had everything under control.

We were about an hour into the sortie established over the target area when I heard this report from my lead sensor operator:

"Pilot, Sensor, I've got a problem. I need to troubleshoot my equipment." Fortunately, I had just finished teaching the co-pilot everything I knew about the sensor system, so the troubleshooting steps were fresh in my mind. I began to fire off a list of items my sensor operator could check to see if we could get the system back online. After about the third suggestion, I heard the sensor operator ask, "Hey, Pilot, I didn't hear you ask the engineer or lead gun a bunch of questions when their systems were broken. Do you not trust me to fix my system? Am I not a professional too?" Wow! What a powerful question. As a leader myself, his response made me feel like a micromanager who did not trust a member of his team. This feeling hurt because those are two of the characteristics I absolutely despise in toxic leadership.

"Colonel, I've got a problem." This experience has stuck with me as I transitioned out of the cockpit and into higher-level leadership roles. As a leader, it is easy not to micromanage when you are not the subject matter expert in a particular area. However, a good leader must maintain the same level of respect to their subordinates if a particular problem falls inside their primary skill set. Forgetting this philosophy can result in fracturing a critical relationship within your team. Always start from the view that everyone on your team is a professional until they prove otherwise. Most likely, you will find out your team already has everything under control. This experience ultimately shaped the cornerstone of my command philosophy.

A commander's priorities need to be made clear to an organization. The message should be concise, easy to understand, and repeatable. Having an easy-to-digest message will allow a leader to consistently repeat it to ensure 100 percent understanding. For my unit, I asked a simple question at the beginning of every commander's call and meeting: "What is the number one rule of the 551st?"

The answer to this question was always a resounding, "The Golden Rule!" Treat others like you want to be treated—with respect. This simple philosophy encompasses almost every facet of our organization. Specifically, it emphasizes the importance of mutual respect, the value of people's time, inclusion, and trust. At the beginning of every tough conversation, leadership challenge, or problem involving a unit or family member, the first question I encouraged my team to ask was, "What is the number one rule?" By following this simple guidance, my team was able to build a healthy unit culture which prevented someone from having to ask, "Am I not a professional too?"

Clarity of Purpose

"Why are you here?" Such a simple, yet extraordinarily powerful question. As the commander of an Air Force Formal Training squadron, this was the first question I'd ask when determining whether I would remove someone from training and potentially help them find an occupation outside the Air Force. At such a critical crossroads in a person's life, knowing the answer to this simple question becomes vitally important.

Usually, the responses to this life-altering inquiry were fairly elementary. I would hear, "I want to serve my country," or, "This job sounds cool," or, "I want to see the world." All of these answers are valid responses, but I can usually satisfy their life-fulfilling desire through another occupation more suited to their individual talents. It can be a hard pill to swallow at the time, but an individual's quality of life is normally significantly better when they are appropriately matched to an occupation fitting their skills, aptitude, and demeanor. However, one particular student gave an answer which absolutely convinced the cadre to keep her in training.

She was asked, "Why do you want to be a gunship sensor operator?" She replied, "I want to stop planting trees." When asked to explain further, she divulged she grew up at Fort Stewart, Georgia, and was in high school during the September 11, 2001 terrorist attacks. She had watched the 3rd Infantry Division deploy to support the war effort. In 2003, leadership at Fort Stewart began planting trees to memorialize soldiers killed in either Iraq or Afghanistan. Today, this memorial is known as Warriors Walk and has 469 trees in the grove. She stated that if her being a sensor operator meant she could help someone come home to their family and one less tree was planted, then she would have done her job. At the time, the gunship sensor career field was one of the few direct action combat occupations available for females in the Air Force. Her clarity of purpose was so focused, the cadre unanimously agreed to keep her in the program. A few months later, we were deployed together, and she was able to fulfill her passion to keep soldiers safe so they could return to their families. It is important for leaders not only to ask the right question, but also to closely listen to the response. Sometimes the simplest questions yield the most moving and powerful answers. So... Why are *you* here?

Astro's Leadership Lessons

1. Respect is the foundation of an organization's culture. The responsibility of setting this culture resides with every member of the organization. It begins every morning with eye contact and a warm salutation, continues throughout the day with consistent team-work, and ends with leadership setting a healthy pace for the unit.

2. Time is your most valuable resource. From the bottom to the top, every member of an organization has the same number of seconds in a day. A leader has the responsibility of cherishing every one of those seconds. If a task is a waste of time, eliminate it and return that time to the member to be with their family.

3. Never say, "No." Instead, ask, "What is the cost?" Almost every request has a solution, but the cost may outweigh the reward. If "No" is the first response, then you may never find out whether "Yes" was an option.

MATTHEW A. "ASTRO" ASTROTH

Colonel Astroth, originally from North Carolina, is a 2000 graduate of the United States Air Force Academy. His command experience includes squadron commander of the 551st Special Operations Squadron at Cannon Air Force Base in New Mexico, mission commander of the 16th Expeditionary Special Operations Squadron in Kuwait, and mission commander of the 4th Special Operations Squadron in Iraq. Additionally, he is an Air Force Command Pilot with over 3,000 flight hours including 1,256 combat hours in the AC-130U and AC-130W gunships, supporting joint and coalition combat operations during Operation Iraqi Freedom, Operation Enduring Freedom, and Operation Inherent Resolve across the Middle East and the Horn of Africa. The culmination of these experiences has shaped his command philosophies of respect, trust, and balancing risk with mission.

Values, Beliefs, and Decision-Making

by Craig S. Bailey

Values, Family, Mistakes, and Recovery

I deeply value family, and I always consider my units family. I also value structure, organization, and accountability, which I've lived by in all three of my squadrons. Whether personal, familial, or professional, I want to know, and I want my team to know, what the expectations and boundaries are. If I cross a line or break a rule, I want to know what price I'll have to pay or what I can expect to happen.

In 2009, I was reassigned to Wright-Patterson Air Force Base in Ohio, about thirty minutes from where I grew up, and I had a *lot* of family nearby. Like most families, mine had endured its fair share of ups and downs, and we were quickly sucked into family drama. One of my nephews was struggling. He had no structure or organization and was getting in trouble. At nineteen years old, he'd been kicked out of the house and was living in his car. When my wife, Lori, and I heard about this, we told him he could stay with us for a couple of weeks to figure things out, but the temporary stay soon became permanent.

We now had three sons, and it wasn't easy. My nephew had basically been allowed to do whatever he wanted for years. He needed a lot of work while he was learning our values. We gave him serious structure and organization, and at nineteen, he finally had clear rules and guidelines and was quickly getting counseled and grounded when he broke them. However, he was also sitting down and eating dinner with family on a regular basis for the first time in years and knew we genuinely cared about him. Over the course of many months, Lori and I worked with my nephew to help him find his way. The path was hard on everyone, and we were mentally and emotionally exhausted, but things eventually worked out. He enjoyed being a part of the family and found that he liked structure and organization. He also understood the importance of accountability. So he decided the military was the right place for him and enlisted in the Army.

Over the last ten years, he's remained a close member of our family. We see him on a regular basis, and he's called to discuss the big decisions in his life. Life has been hard on him, but he's always continued to push forward. Now, he's an outstanding father to his sons and doing great in the Army as an E-6. He's lived one heck of a life and has some great stories to tell his soldiers as he leads and mentors them.

In 2012, I took command of the 51st Munitions Squadron at Osan Air Base in Korea. I loved the mission and the squadron, which quickly became family to me. Osan was very busy. It was forty-eight miles from North Korea, and the wing was always flexing its muscles demonstrating we were ready to fight tonight. We preached and lived our values of family, structure, organization, and accountability, and this was immediately impressed on new arrivals. We built a lot of ammo, generated a lot of aircraft, and were exercising all the time. The team knew that they would be working hard during their tour in Korea, and like anywhere else, when you work hard, you tend to play hard. Seoul was only thirty miles away and a great place to party, and Songtan, the town outside base, seemed to have a club or bar every fifty feet. Needless to say, alcohol-related incidents (ARIs) were a regular occurrence for Airmen, so Senior Leadership established a 1 a.m. curfew in an effort to curb them. During my command, I served fourteen Article 15s, or non-judicial punishments, eleven of which were for ARIs or curfew violations.

We had a critical mission—to be ready at any time to provide ammo for the fight. My team knew the expectations, both on and off-duty. They also understood that if they failed to meet expectations, they would be held accountable. ARIs and curfew violations were "absolute nots," and violating either almost always led to non-judicial punishment and the loss of a stripe, or demotion. Late in 2013, one of my Staff Sergeant (SSgt) Munitions Line-Delivery drivers was arrested for a curfew violation. He was a solid Airman, had never been in trouble, and did a great work. He came into my office and said, "Sir, I messed up. No excuse. I know I'm going to lose my stripe." But I had another problem. He was a ten-year SSgt If I took a stripe, he'd be a High Year Tenure Senior Airman, and the same way my nephew was kicked out of the family home, this SSgt would get kicked out of the Air Force.

After lengthy discussions with the team, everything kept coming back to accountability, and ultimately, good order and discipline for the unit. Folks knew the expectations and the price to be paid if you crossed the line. It was a difficult decision, but I took the stripe. My Airman didn't bat an eye. He asked if he could stand in front of the squadron and make sure the unit knew what happened in the hopes of preventing the next ARI or curfew violation. Even though he knew his days in the Air Force were numbered, he didn't let up at work. I was extremely impressed by his maturity and how he was dealing with this.

Weeks later, I found myself in a conversation with one of the Airman's friends. He told me that the Airman had received a text from his wife the night of the curfew violation informing him that she wanted a divorce. I was blown away and even more impressed that my Airman hadn't brought up the text or tried to use it as an excuse when I was handing down his punishment. He just kept saying, "I messed up, I own it, and I expect to pay the price." Bottom line, the additional information I received weighed heavily on me.

My First Sergeant and I did some research to see what we could do for our Airman. We found that I could mitigate a portion of the punishment if the member's good conduct after the incident merited the mitigation. Our Airman had made a mistake, he had owned it, and he had been held accountable. I felt the additional information I had received, coupled with his exemplary conduct and job performance post-violation, warranted the mitigation. My leadership team agreed that he deserved a second chance, and I gave him his SSgt stripe back.

This Airman continues to thrive. Since his incident in 2013, he's made Technical Sergeant and Master Sergeant. I recently spoke with him, and he continues to be incredibly grateful and appreciative of his second chance, and he uses it as an example for his Airmen. He was recently selected to be a First Sergeant, and I have no doubt he'll do an outstanding job.

Family, structure, organization, and accountability have been stabilizing factors in my squadrons and were critical to good order and discipline. Over the course of my twenty-nine years in the Air Force, I've worked with countless Airmen. Unfortunately, many of them made mistakes. As I deliberated and decided how I would hold them accountable, I always reminded myself that these Airmen are part of my family. The vast majority of them, when offered a little guidance, help, and support, have worked hard to overcome their mistakes, and succeed.

Troops in Contact

Over my last twenty-nine years in the Air Force, I've found that if you truly care for and treat people like family, they perform better and will do everything possible to make the mission happen. I've also operated using the following beliefs during my service:

1. Airmen must understand their roles, responsibilities, and how their efforts contribute to the mission. When our Airmen understand how they fit in, it's almost always accompanied by an increase in performance, job satisfaction, and pride.

2. Great units are full of motivated Airmen who have passion for what they do. They love their job, enjoy the challenge, and thrive on the sense of service. They are excited and driven, and they believe their work and efforts make a difference. Without passion and motivation, some Airmen put in minimal effort and perform the job because they have to, or just to collect a paycheck, and can leave passionate and motivated co-workers wondering why they should continue working hard.

3. Every job in the unit serves an end user or customer. We wouldn't be here without our mission or customers. Performing our jobs in a manner to meet customer needs and mission requirements is part of our ethical responsibility. If we do not produce or provide the service the mission requires or that our

customer expects or needs, we may find ourselves without customers, or possibly a job.

4. The unit must always be ready to respond to the challenges that may come. This means developing and mentoring Airmen with formal and informal training to meet mission requirements in normal and adverse conditions. This also means leaders must get out from behind the desk. The place of business is out where the action or mission is. We need to see and understand what's going on within our span of control. Airmen will see that we're interested in their problems, working conditions, and welfare.

5. Don't put off hard decisions because you're not willing to make them today. This doesn't mean making impulsive or unreasonable decisions just to be prompt. But once you've assessed all inputs and have arrived at what you believe is right, be decisive, and get on with it.

6. Good leaders clearly identify the results they expect, then support their Airmen and help them achieve those results. Results are benchmarks and lessons for the future as well as goals for the present. Ethics factor into results. We don't pursue results at any cost. We must understand our mission, our available resources, and our capabilities, then assess risk and work toward desired results while maintaining our values.

7. Airmen in great units have the will to persist and keep working even when results are not what they expected. Their persistence is tied to their passion and a belief that the squadron will be successful. So they work harder, assessing

and accepting risk while maintaining honor and integrity. They maintain customer focus and always strive to meet mission requirements. As leaders, we must ensure our Airmen understand the importance of values and tie them to our strategies, plans, and decisions. While persistence to meet mission requirements is highly desired, our Airmen need to clearly understand what's allowed, what's not allowed, and who the decision-making authority is for accepting risks when they're pushing hard to get the results we want.

In 2005, I became the Officer-in-Charge of the 75th Aircraft Maintenance Unit (AMU) at Pope Air Force Base in North Carolina. We were part of the 23rd Fighter Group and the World-Famous Flying Tigers. The unit consisted of 220 Airmen to maintain twenty-two A-10s and generate sorties for the 75th Fighter Squadron. I loved being a part of the Flying Tigers. I loved the A-10 and the critical mission we supported with our Fighter Squadron. I loved the tiger teeth on the nose of our aircraft. And most importantly, I loved the 75th AMU family. I had a hard-charging Lieutenant and three kick-ass Senior Master Sergeants I referred to as "the three-headed dream team" to help me lead and manage operations across the AMU. We generated about 300 sorties producing around 600 flying hours each month. Our fleet of A-10s averaged twenty-five years, and they were really showing their age. At the same time, like most other AMUs across the Air Force, we had a rather young maintenance team with an average age younger than our A-10 fleet.

When I arrived, the AMU was struggling and came in second... out of two A-10 AMUs. There were things I wanted to try to improve performance. I had a discussion with my Squadron Commander and asked permission for some scheduling and management changes. He liked my ideas and said, "Craig, it's your AMU. I trust you to do what you see fit."

Great! I thought. *I'll press on with my changes,* and *my boss trusts me!*

About a month later, I was back in my Commander's office to talk about some more things I wanted to do. He cut me off in the middle of the discussion and said something to the effect of, "Craig, I told you it's your AMU. Keep doing the things you're doing. I'll let you know if I have a problem with it."

Wow, this is cool! My boss implicitly trusts me and has totally empowered me to lead the AMU... again! I was thinking, *Glad I have my three-headed dream team to help me, because we were busy!* I also loved my job. I knew every day would be a ten to twelve-hour day, but I still looked forward to it.

We were less than twelve months out from a fourteen-ship deployment to Bagram, Afghanistan, and we had an Air Combat Command (ACC) Operational Readiness Inspection (ORI) coming up within four months. We also had three large-package off-station spin-up exercises to participate in, a joint training with ground units so our pilots could hone their skills in close air support—a twelve-ship to Barksdale for Green Flag-East, a twelve-ship to Nellis for Air Warrior, and a twelve-ship to Red Flag-Alaska. During all of this, we still needed to produce 300 monthly sorties to keep our fighter squadron mission-ready.

Things quickly started to trend in a positive direction. We established a Tiger Team and started scrutinizing our aging fleet. On average, we identified and corrected thirty discrepancies per aircraft, and it worked. Within three months, our mission-capable rate for our A-10 fleet soared to 88 percent, meaning on any given day, we had about nineteen A-10s ready to fly and take care of business. Our repeat/recur rate for aircraft problems identified by pilots was cut to 2 percent. This meant our maintainers were doing great troubleshooting on the aircraft, identifying the root cause to repair the problem. Better yet, our ground abort rate was cut to 1.4 percent. This meant that out of 300 monthly sorties, we had to use a spare aircraft to replace a broken one an average of only four times. Our efforts were also validated by a steady rise in Quality Assurance pass rates for our maintainers and a 50 percent reduction in the number of safety and technical data violations. Pride and morale across the AMU were also on the rise, and the team was winning two out of three "AMU of the Month" awards. At this point, maintainers from our sister AMU were even asking if they could come over to our team.

There were some major obstacles on the road to deployment. In January 2006, the ACC Inspector General (IG) arrived for our ORI. Our sister AMU was evaluated on aircraft generation (preparing aircraft and launching them for wartime deployment), and my AMU was evaluated on aircraft regeneration (receiving and reconfiguring aircraft for wartime operations). Our sister AMU honestly had the tougher of the two tasks. While we received an "Excellent" for the regeneration aspect, the generation effort of our sister AMU was unfortunately rated "Unsatisfactory." This meant we had to redo the aircraft generation portion of our ORI in July, and not just that. Group leadership decided I would lead efforts for the ORI generation redo with my AMU because they felt more confident in our team. *What? Did I hear that right?* My first thought was, *Are you f*cking kidding me?* We were deploying in September and still had the Air Warrior and Red Flag-Alaska exercises to manage, which were lengthy trips and required a lot of prep. I couldn't sleep at all the night I heard this. It wasn't easy, but things came together, and we made it through. Both exercises went off without a hitch, and we met every objective. We also successfully made it through the ORI redo with stellar marks.

As the deployment crept closer, we were dealing with a backlog of upgrades and training for new pilots. Unfortunately, we were even at work the weekend prior to our deployment completing the final upgrades. I'll never forget the deployment launch-out. It seemed like anything that could go wrong, went wrong. Half of our jets had maintenance issues during launch. We went through all of our spare aircraft but eventually got our required fourteen aircraft and 250 Airmen from Pope to Bagram. When I landed in Bagram, it honestly felt good to be there. I knew I'd miss my family terribly, but my team had gone through one of the busiest years on record prior to the deployment. Up to that point, it was the absolute busiest year I'd had in the Air Force.

Our main mission in Afghanistan was to support troops on the ground and "Troops in Contact" with the enemy. Our main customers were the soldiers from the 10th Mountain Division. We wanted every jet available when called upon. This meant doing a lot of prep work prior to the deployment. We scrounged for manpower and set up an additional phase dock to conduct lengthy two-week major inspections on our A-10s. This helped us bank an additional 560 flying hours to use in theater. We also completed a large amount of scheduled maintenance early, eliminating 30 percent of the time-consuming maintenance in theater. We did whatever we could to support the joint team. During the deployment, we even completed a major modification of our A-10s and equipped them with ARC-210 radios to enable direct communication between our pilots and ground troops.

Our efforts paid off. We had three aircraft on alert to respond to Troops in Contact within twelve hours of arrival. During the five-month deployment, we conducted fifty-two alert launches and averaged a fifteen-minute takeoff from initial notification. The standard in the Area of Responsibility (AOR) was thirty minutes from the initial call for help. We generally had four to six aircraft airborne at any given time. My team was incredible, as were the results of the deployment. We generated 2,000 sorties and 7,600 flight hours in a five-month period with   fourteen A-10s. Keep in mind, at Pope, we generated 7,200 flight hours with twenty-two A-10s *for an entire year!* Our aircrews expended 79,000 munitions (30mm ammo, rockets, air-to-ground missiles, and bombs), eliminating more than 400 enemy soldiers during the deployment.

There was one day in late October 2006 that I will always remember. Late that morning, we launched two alert A-10s in support of a ten-man Army team and an Afghan National Army (ANA) team engaged with an estimated 100 to 150 Taliban fighters. The four A-10s that were already airborne also answered the call for help. We now had six A-10s airborne supporting the team. Within thirty minutes, we had two more A-10s generated and airborne. This continued over and over until every available A-10 was airborne, either supporting the Troops in Contact or returning from the engagement to be quick-turned and sent back to the fight. Every A-10 returning was coming back with all weapons and ammo expended. Our pilots could visibly see and hear the anxiety in the voices of our soldiers under heavy fire and completely surrounded by and in close proximity to the enemy on the ground. Ops asked us to do whatever we could to turn the aircraft as quickly as possible. Our returning pilots jumped out of the jets saying they were engaging the enemy between fifty and 100 feet from the ground because our forces were so close to the enemy. They said they may have even hit the treetops and asked us to look hard for any battle damage from enemy fire.

That day, we did things different from how we had ever done them before. More than anything else, the resource I needed most was time. The only way to make up time was to do things we would never do in a peacetime environment. What we were doing was similar to old-school integrated combat turns. We knowingly violated tech data and committed safety violations to turn the aircraft as fast as we could to get our A-10s back to combat. It looked like a NASCAR pit crew on the aircraft. We had crew chiefs on the top and bottom, inspecting, servicing, and refueling. Once the fuel truck was out of the way, two weapons load crews joined the party and were simultaneously loading bombs, rockets, and 30mm ammo with the pilot waiting to jump back into the cockpit. The process that would normally take one-and-a-half to two hours on good day was taking twenty-five to thirty minutes. My leadership team and I were closely overseeing operations, keeping things as safe as we could. The maintenance team was incredibly focused and in the zone. Strangely, it didn't seem chaotic at all. In fact, it seemed well-choreographed and looked like something we'd been doing for a long time. The team understood they were making exceptions they would never make in peacetime, but only because the situation warranted it, and our teammates on the ground under fire needed help.

When the day was over, the entire team beamed with pride and knew the significance of what they'd done. This was exactly the kind of thing we were there for. The battle that day lasted nearly six hours and resulted in fifty-five enemy killed in action and twenty enemy wounded. Unfortunately, we also lost an Army brother during the battle.

Craig's Leadership Lessons

I will never take an unnecessary risk. That day, we were the 911 response team. I assessed the situation and assumed the risk because bullets were flying at our Army and ANA teammates on the ground. The entire team was eager to do whatever it took to support those in harm's way. I knew that if something went wrong, I would be held accountable, but I'd do it again in a heartbeat.

As leaders, we are given authority and responsibility to lead and manage personnel and operations and make the tough decisions, especially when the chips are down, and things aren't going as planned. So my leadership lesson is this: When hard decisions must be made, assess the situation, consult your team, and be decisive. This also means you'd better know and understand your job, your mission, your resources, your priorities, and your team's capabilities. Do your homework and make the tough call in a timely manner.

CRAIG S. BAILEY

Colonel Bailey enlisted in the Air Force in 1991 and earned his commission through Officer Training School in August 2000. He has led maintenance efforts for fighter, bomber, and rescue aircraft, as well as conventional and nuclear munitions. Col Bailey has deployed in support of Operation Iraqi Freedom and Operation Enduring Freedom. He has served as Commander for the 51st Munitions Squadron, Osan AB, Korea, the 355th Equipment Maintenance Squadron, Davis-Monthan AFB, Arizona, and the 701st Munitions Support Squadron, Kleine-Brogel, Belgium. He is married to Lori Bailey, née Bancroft, and they have two sons, Brandon and Brett. Col Bailey holds a B.S. in Professional Aeronautics and a Master of Aeronautical Science, both from Embry-Riddle Aeronautical University, and a M.S. in Logistics from Air Force Institute of Technology.

God Plants a Garden

by Demetrius N. Booth

Adorned in Love

If I speak with the tongues of angels, and know all mysteries and knowledge, but do not have Love… I am nothing.
    –1 Corinthians 13

Tapestries of their Sunday best, familiar faces coupled with warm embraces, welcome all who bound beyond the threshold. We have come to this place to honor the passage of time, to immortalize moments with song, prayer, and the delivery of speeches. Memories are frozen in pictures and stand as monuments to the continuous shedding of time from this world. Joyful, quiet, sad, somber, loved, contented, lost. There are no strangers here. I stand holding my younger brother's hand, who at six-foot-two towers over my five-foot-eight frame. This journey is the longest we have ever taken, pews filled with watchful eyes gazing upon our strength.

It was twenty-five years earlier when I learned my most valued lesson—the meaning of love without condition. My brother, Lil Wes, and I had different fathers. I have a distant memory of when he would head out for a weekend to spend time with his dad, and I would wait endlessly for mine to show up. My whole life, I had been told that John was my father, which left me to imagine what it would be like to have him in my life. On one of those fateful weekends, my brother returned from a visit with his dad. Once he understood that I had spent another weekend with my mother and younger sisters, he offered to share his father with me. As a matter of fact, it happened just like that: "I will share my dad with you," he said. "My dad will be your dad too." Initially, I dismissed the notion, thinking to myself, you can't share a dad. Besides, what if he didn't want another son, or what if he didn't want me around?

Lil Wesley was undeterred. As his father arrived to pick him up, he informed Wesley, Sr., affectionately called Big Wes, that I would be his son too. Big Wes agreed, much to my surprise, and off the three of us went into the sunset. I forged an inseparable bond with Big Wes; he became my father, and I was his son. I witnessed Big Wes dance with my mother in the street to music played on the car radio while my brother smiled. I can still hear him say, "Georgia Ann, you supposed to be my wife." He would kiss Lil Wes and me on the cheek and hug us even after we were grown and had children of our own. When we would try to fight it, he would remind us that we were his babies, and he could kiss us all he wanted. Big Wes stood a slender six-foot-one, walked on his tippy toes as if he was floating away, and had a personality that would light up a room. Lil Wes and I looked forward to the moments we could spend with our dad. His energy was enough to hold us over until we could see him again. But for all the love that God had poured into Big Wes before he reached Earth, he had come with personal demons as well. His drink of choice, Wild Irish Rose, would consume him just as much as he consumed it. At the end of each bottle, this fallen angel found himself distant from the peace he experienced on weekends when his sons were present. We were the safe space on Earth where he was never judged for being human.

Lil Wes and I witnessed the struggles of addiction and the triumph of the spirit by watching our dad live a life fraught with obstacles, hurt, passion, love, sadness, and joy. We would go for long stints without seeing our dad as he fumbled through life. My mother would do the work to find out where he was staying and make sure he was presentable for our young hearts to see. I imagine that this withered her soul. As teenagers, she drove us in protest to see him. Once, he emerged from a basement apartment thinner than we remembered, a few of his teeth missing, and his eye was swollen to the point that it looked as if the pressure would dislodge it from his skull, and the earth seemed to give way just a little with each step toward us. We found out that his addiction to drugs had led him to steal from his cousin, who in turn had sought a pound of flesh as payment to ensure it would never happen again. We couldn't stay with him this weekend; it was an unsuitable environment even for an adult. Our mother's bearlike instinct to protect her cubs forced us back into the car. As we drove off, Lil Wes and I looked toward the rear window to see him fade away into the distance alone.

A few years passed, and my mother's investigative skills proved formidable yet again as she found him, this time doing very well, married to our now-stepmother and with two more children. As it was with me, his love recognized no boundaries. These two souls, who had not come from him, still belonged to him. Lil Wes and I were jealous; we had formed a triad. Who did he think he was to be doing well and married with two more children? He should have been saving his best for us. The air in the room was thick as he introduced us to our new little sister and brother. Big Wes was so proud as he listed his children in order by age: "I got a tough squad... DeeDee, JohnJohn, Lil Wes, and Jellybean." But my heart couldn't match his visible smile. Noticing the discontentment between Lil Wes and me, he decided to take us for a walk. The Earth's gravity could hardly hold him in place as he walked on his tippy toes, laughing, and speaking to everyone in the neighborhood. Even people he didn't know would yell out, "Hey, Big Wes!" and he would reply, "Whoop... What ya doin' now!" During our walk, he expressed love, talked about JohnJohn and Jellybean, and poured love into Lil Wes and me with still more to give. He hadn't replaced us; he'd set the environment for us to be dressed in even more love.

We are wonderfully made and yet mortal in all things. The calm San Antonio air was disrupted by a phone call. My stepmother asked me where my wife was and what I was doing. Her calling wasn't unusual because we spoke often, and each year when I would visit home, she was a main stop. Once she knew my wife was in the room, she broke the news that my father had passed. The man who rode his bike to work each day, struggled with alcoholism, and lived life full of love had died from a massive heart attack. Big Wes had the biggest heart in the world from my vantage point and I couldn't understand her words. How could the strongest heart I know give out?

I squeezed Lil Wes' hand and said, "Let's go say thank you to our dad." His feet broke free of the weights that had been holding him in place, just as my presence comforted him to start the journey. I took the first step, but his stride quickly caught up to mine, and we walked together as we have always done to usher our dad into his place of peace in this world, devoid of judgment and full of love.

It has been ten years since Wesley, Sr., transitioned to a place beyond our understanding, but my stepmother is still a main stop when we go home. She is a part of my life that seems to have never been introduced. My brother is now called Big Wes and has ten children, including his eldest son, Lil Wes. Jellybean now has a daughter of her own, and I love her the way Big Wes would have. I dance in the street with my wife, much to her embarrassment, and I kiss my own children every day. There are dances in the living room, there is always room for ice cream, and there is no moment I don't say I love you. This book's pages aren't sturdy enough to hold the life of Big Wes. Other than expressing the love he poured over me, I am unworthy to tell his story alone. Countless lives are better because they knew him, and I count myself blessed that he had chosen to spend moments of his life with me.

Cultivate the Garden

You must understand the whole of life, not just one part of it.
    –Krishnamurti

"You look like William." For the first thirty-six years of my life, I did not know my biological father. Where I am from, a young black kid not knowing his father is an unwelcome staple. This hood status comes with jokes from other kids whose fathers were present in their lives and daydreams of fantasy fathers coming to the rescue, only to be forced to confront the inevitable truth that we are figuring out this world from a fallen state. There persists this awkwardness in my adult life when a physician asks about my father's medical history. My steady and confident response, usually something like, "I do not know my father," often leaves more questions than I have answers for. The truth is, my response really means I don't know who I am. There are shadowy areas of my soul for which I have only part of an answer, or none at all, to explain.

Yet the horrors of the shade of those shadowy places found me exiting my vehicle to finally meet the man who helped with my existence. This day had been coming for more than thirty-six years. We were unconnected in any way....until my wife came to me and said, "I found your father." My wife is my high school sweetheart, and one of the few people we had stayed in touch with from those days was now a part of the police department and turned out to be friends with both my wife and my father on social media.

After several drinks to muster my courage, I sent a message. "My name is Demetrius. You don't know me, but you knew my mother. I have been told that you are my father, so I wanted to reach out and speak with you. I hope you are up for it, but if not, I understand."

The area code from our hometown flashed across the caller ID, the man on the phone asked for me, and my wife passed me the phone. "Is this Demetrius?" a voice asked.

I replied, "Yes?"

His response, "This is William."

My heart felt as if it had gotten stuck in my throat. Most of what was spoken is still a blur to me, but he asked to see me the next time I was home. I informed him that I would be traveling back in a few weeks, and we made plans to meet. I had grown up in a tight-knit family; there wasn't a weekend when my brother, sisters, and I did not spend the night at a cousin's house or them at ours. Once William passed me his address, I realized that it was five city blocks away from where I'd spent most of my weekends growing up. It's funny how we can spend a lifetime exploring the world to find answers that send us right back to where we started.

I didn't go looking for a person to be a father to me; I went because I needed to know myself. Only by understanding who he is can I know who I am. It was this man's light that would illuminate those shadowy areas in my soul, thus illuminating my identity and, in the words of Marian Williamson, send me toward a path of returning to love.

I sat in a chair across from a mirror image of myself, possibly looking into the future, and he looked back into the past. I noticed our hand gestures, the way our legs crossed as we spoke, his nose, that smile that my daughter had gotten from me… we'd both gotten it from him. I found myself adjusting my posture and my mannerisms when I spoke, specifically not to mimic this man. How could this be? How did I absorb so much of this person without knowing him? The three hours we spent together were unbound by the constraints of time. It flew by and lasted forever. It was everything and nothing at all. He left me with three cautions about myself. I now understood who I was, but more importantly, I had work to do. We took a photo together. For him, it was proof for his sister that I looked like him; for me, it was a record that I do, in fact, exist.

Letters to Myself

The one who does the work does the learning.
   –Terry Doley

I cannot go back in time to right wrongs, give myself advice to help with the present, or to provide comfort during hard times. But as I look at my own mirrored image and consider who I was and what advice I needed from a father when I had none, I see Demetrius, Jr., looking right back at me. So I decided to write letters to my younger self as a current father in consideration of the life I'd lived in front of my son up to that point. In these letters, I have set out on a journey to prepare him with the tools I did not have, tools for the world he will live in, a world that does not quite exist yet. Below are some examples.

Letter #1: It doesn't get any easier, but we do get better.

We get better when we do the work, and the work is required every day. Math was never a strength of mine. I didn't put much effort into learning the language, so I struggled to keep pace with my classmates. I saw my son suffering the same fate and took steps to intervene. There were moments when he was so frustrated that tears flowed. There were times when he danced in triumph because for once, he was the kid with all the answers. It was in his triumph that Letter #1 became the most important. DJ had not mastered essential steps, and I knew that it would cause problems for him later. This feeling was prophetic as he began to work on long division. In the weeks between multiplication and long division, DJ's confidence was at an all-time high. He failed to practice his multiplication each day. He began to feel that it was easy as he danced in front of the whiteboard full of math problems, but this confidence would come crashing down as he had to incorporate multiplications in his process to work long division math problems. His response to me while in tears was, "It was easy last week." It was in this moment that it hit me. I sat next to him and said, "Son, it never gets easy. For someone else, the thing you mastered today was their stumbling block. The math wasn't easier last week; you were better. You were better because you did the work, and the work is required every day."

Letter #2: If you want it, you've got to work for it.

I grew up in the heyday of Chicago basketball in the 1990s, when the Bulls ruled the court and His Airness, Michael Jordan, was considered the greatest player to lace up a pair of basketball shoes. It was my love for the Bulls that caused me to collect basketball cards, but at the time, I was too young to gain full-time employment to support my habit. My mother worked to provide the essential things, and cards did not make the list each month. I remember visiting my cousin Cory for the weekend. We asked his father, Ira, for money to catch the train to the mall and to buy basketball cards. Uncle Ira walked us to the basement, showed us a shovel and a bag of rock salt, and told us to make money to buy the things we wanted. If we were going to purchase a pack of cards to add to our growing collection, we would need to convince the neighbors that they needed to hire us to shovel their sidewalks.

It was one of the coldest winters in Chicago history, at least that's how Cory, my brother Wesley, and I remember it. We must have shoveled the sidewalks for twelve of the neighbors, covering three city blocks. Finally, we had earned enough to get the basketball cards we wanted. Our fulfilled desire was sweet to our souls, but more importantly, we had done it ourselves—not our parents, and not with handouts. We had worked hard and had reaped the spoils of our labor. My son would also find himself in similar circumstances. I would walk into the bedroom and overhear him asking his mother again for money to purchase items on one of his video games. I disrupted his plan by telling my wife that she could not give him money, but mandate that he should do extra chores to earn it. I proposed to pay minimum wage for each hour of work he performed. DJ earned the money he needed, purchased his items, and felt the same pride I had many years prior.

I have written many more letters to my son. I am not proud of all of them, but when he looks back at my writing, I hope he sees better than bad. My acts of living a purpose-aligned life are my manifesto to him. I hope these letters to him will resonate in his heart as he paves the way for his own children, that these letters will act as a beacon to guide him to being better man than I ever could have hoped to be, that he knows I love him, and that I remain a safe space to land on when he is triumphant, bruised, or tired.

What I Run Toward

She didn't know whether she was running away from something or running to something, but she admitted that deep in her heart she wanted to go home.
    –Beatrice Sparks, from *Go Ask Alice*

I had gotten into an argument with my wife regarding something, but as I think back, I can't remember what it was. Most of our skirmishes happen this way. I figured a run would clear my head and getting out of the house in some way would resolve the problem. I had marked off a 3.2-mile figure-eight loop in our subdivision. The moment I took off running, the very second step of my stride untimely started to bring me right back.

Shortly after the horrific attacks of September 11, 2001, I was stationed in South Korea. It was the height of the war, and being a security specialist, I wanted to do my part. That would have to wait a year because I was needed for the end strength in Korea.

The run did not take me away from my problems. I was still immersed in them. The entire time, I played back what had happened in my head and thought through what I should have said. In some moments, I was angrier; in others, I felt that it wasn't worth the energy. All of it is a matter of perspective. People who run from their problems tend to have to face them in the end. I have seen leaders time and time again pretend, hide, or turn a blind eye to problems. And I don't mean to cast the first stone as if I have not suffered this laissez-faire leadership style in my past. If the layers of the situation are pulled back and issues are seen from above instead of inside, we might realize the gunfire is coming regardless. There is a choice to be made—face it or have it catch up to you later, but either way, soon enough, you will be forced to deal with it.

I remember our Commander saying during a Commander's Call, "The one thing that sets us apart is when the shots are fired, while the sheep are running away, we, the sheepdogs, are running toward the threat. That takes a crazy kind of person to run into harm's way, and I am glad I found y'all. I couldn't imagine running into the battle by myself." This message spoke to me on a deep level. This was the true embodiment of courage—to know that harm, pain, torment, or even death is ahead, but still be willing to move toward it anyway.

I still think back to that analogy of the sheep and sheepdog, but now I wonder what it is that the sheep are running to. Is it temporary comfort, a façade of safety, the place where cold, timid souls go, or perhaps the notion of living to fight another day? As a leader, I have learned to choose to use my energy to run toward the gunfire of sub-par performance, injustice, uncomfortable conversations, inequality, and so much more, and to face them all with the courage required to speak truth to power. Because the standards we ignore become the standards we accept. If we muster the courage to face our fears in the process, we liberate others and restore order. It's not about legacy; it's about the impact, and the true impact lives just beyond "what's in it for me." Using our light for good starts the process to heal the fractured world.

D's Leadership Lessons

1. At the beginning of the Judeo-Christian tradition, God speaks the world into existence, and then plants a garden and places Adam there to cultivate it. I've learned that this garden is a metaphor for life. This is our first vocation—life is given, and it is our responsibility to cultivate it. We must weed out the bad, water the good, and prune out hate.

2. Extraordinary lives are never extinguished. While death is a part of the natural process of life, love is the great equalizer. It is love that brings us here, love that sustains us, and love that makes life worth living. To restore order, you must choose to love.

3. The path begins with a return to loving yourself. Then it continues toward the work of leaving a love letter behind to the world because there is nothing more potent than love, not even death.

DEMETRIUS N. BOOTH

Demetrius Booth hails from the South Side of Chicago, where he was born and raised. He has served in the United States Air Force for twenty years. He has a dialogical-xenosophia approach to life and religion and wants to be known for being a lighthouse for others navigating the darkness. Believing that teaching is a part of his purpose, he uses his gifts to heal this fractured world one person at a time. He has been married to his wife, Marilyn, for twenty-two years, and they have four beautiful souls, Nia, Imani, Niama, and Demetrius, Jr., that they have gifted to the world. Booth is a Chief Master Sergeant in the Air Force, has a B.A. in Business Management, and is nearly finished with his master's degree.

Leading with the Head, Heart, and Hands

by Douglas Freeman

It's Not Just You; It's Me, as Well. It's All of Us!

I am an Air Force brat, the son of a retired Air Force Master Sergeant, Lawrence Olden Freeman. However, unlike my older sister, I didn't get to experience the military brat lifestyle—traveling the world, switching schools, and calling everywhere home. There's about a fifteen-year age gap between my sister and me. After being born in Angeles City in the Philippines in 1976, my family moved to Montgomery, Alabama, for my dad's last tour of active duty. My first memories are of riding my big wheel around base housing on what was then Gunter Air Force Station.

I grew up in the Deep South, my dad African American, my mom Filipino. After my dad retired from active duty, he took a civil service job at Maxwell Air Force Base. We moved into a townhome near the cow pastures and ponds of the southeast part of town. I stood out among my peers as a child—dark, tanned skin in the summertime, with thick, black wavy hair. Montgomery in the 1980s and '90s was extremely segregated, so much so that I was part of the Minority-to-Majority school program in an attempt to further desegregate schools from the previous Jim Crow era of the state. To put things into perspective, it would have been illegal for me to marry my white college girlfriend in the State of Alabama until the year 2000.

From the time kids could pick teams at recess, I vividly remember *not* fitting in—being excluded from every group in school. I was neither accepted by black students nor white students. Kids labeled me as Chinese, Japanese, or Mexican as television was their only point of reference for cultures outside the state. I felt alone and hopeless at times, but always felt welcome and accepted when my parents brought me back onto Maxwell. I was able to get along with almost all the other kids at the base pool and the rec center. I always felt a sense of belonging inside the base gates. When I was back off base, I did my best to blend into whatever backdrop lay behind me, often changing the way I dressed and talked to mimic whomever I could spend time with.

My high school years were different—not great, but different. I had decent grades in junior high and elected to attend a nationally acclaimed magnet high school. The idea of sides, cliques, and race were all put aside and replaced by five hours of homework every night. Our common enemy was our course load, and we all were united to overcome it. It was the first time I had gone to class with kids from a variety of other races and backgrounds. Many of those enrolled were children of active-duty members spending one to three years at Maxwell. We shared similar values and a longing to belong.

I began to find some confidence in who I was. I played on my varsity soccer team and participated in various school clubs and civic organizations. I was beginning to make a name for myself, fitting in without blending, but I still could not escape the bitter truth of the culture of my city. The girl I had dated throughout my entire high school career was white and had to hide from her parents the fact that I wasn't. They would have never allowed a black face in the household, let alone a half-Black, half-Filipino one. I have never understood why people think or act the way they do, especially toward someone they barely know.

My college years were spent an hour north at the "Loveliest Village on the Plains," Auburn University. I spent the next four and a half years as part of the Auburn family, as something greater than myself. I spent the majority of my time with my friends who had joined me from Montgomery, and with my ROTC detachment. My college years were the first time I felt somewhat comfortable in my own skin. I graduated from Auburn in fall of 1998 and began my Air Force career shortly afterward.

I still view my life in the Air Force as my salvation, my emancipation from the Deep South and into a life much greater than I could imagine creating on my own. After my initial skills training, I went off to my first duty station, Incirlik Air Base, Turkey. I found myself struggling to adjust to my new lifestyle. I was the only non-white company grade officer in my unit, so I did what I always did—I blended in to find acceptance. Halfway through my tour, I met the woman of my dreams. We dated for the remainder of our time in Turkey, and we were eventually both assigned to Fort Meade, Maryland, where we were married in 2002. My wife just so happens to be white, of English and Irish decent, with beautiful freckles on her face and arms.

As I'm writing this, I'm proud to say I have served twenty-two years in the Air Force. My wife has served twenty-six. We have absolutely loved our time in the service. Our time in the Air Force has been rich and rewarding. I've always seen hard work pay off. While I never bore witness to the sort of racism that our Chief of

Staff of the Air Force, General Charles Brown, made mention of before he took command, my wife and I did see more subtle inequities during our service. For example, if my wife and I were standing together alongside another white male officer, people would assume she was married to him while introductions were being made. This didn't make me angry, but it never sat well with me. I continued to do my best to blend in and not to upset the apple cart.

My wife and I recently moved back to the Montgomery area so she could attend Air War College. I was back in my hometown, but this time with my own family. Our two girls, who both share our best traits, made this trip back to the Deep South quite a different experience for us. Both school-age children, we opted to enroll them in public school in a nearby county that was known for being a better alternative to the failing Montgomery school system. I was lucky enough to land a job at the Air Force Leader Development Course for Squadron Command, a one-year instructional journey through the messy, human domain side of command. My tour has been an amazing journey of self-reflection and exploration. Outside of command, this has been the most rewarding tour of my career, and I've never felt more comfortable in my own skin.

However, I have seen reminders of our past in our local community. Our first week in town, I took the family out to eat while we were still getting settled in our new home. We ate at a local sports pub, enjoying our meal and talking about what our future might bring. When we asked for the check, the waitress asked if we were together or separate. This time it really angered me—a family of four, eating, laughing, and enjoying a meal wouldn't present itself as "together"? I was convinced it was because of the color of my skin. I again could not understand why a person would see the world that way.

When the school year started, our kids would often tell us

stories of their time in their new school. My heart sank as I heard them say that they weren't really fitting in with any of the school groups, that the school was very racially divided, and that their tanned skin, long, straight hair, and military brat vocabulary was pushing them out from acceptance. They were called many of the same names I'd been called in the '80s and '90s. When we spoke to the school administration, we were told it was because the kids were simply curious and hadn't seen many like them before. I wondered if anything could ever change.

A few months later, I went to pick up my future gymnast daughter from the Prattville YMCA, an amazing gymnastics facility and program. My wife usually handles pickup duties, but due to her Air War College schedule, it was my turn. I stood just off the gym floor with the other parents waiting for my daughter to finish up. As I watched for my daughter to appear among the departing little level-four gymnastics group, my eyes locked onto one of her teammates, a tiny black girl. My eyes followed her across the gym to her father, a white man and fellow Air Force officer I had spoken to before. I quickly realized that I had been unconsciously looking for a black father who didn't exist. I then hung my head in shame—had I just done that? Did I just do the same thing that had outraged me my entire life? Then I wondered, *What else have I not realized I've been doing over the years?*

I did so without hate or malice or racial bias—the things my eyes and mind had been trained to see over the past forty-four years. I did so before a backdrop of what I'd been used to seeing in the towns and restaurants I'd been raised in—primarily black or white families in black or white spaces. If this happened to me, someone who has been outraged by racism and has fought to be included his whole life, I wondered who else it might be happening to. I began to wonder how others saw me, and how their eyes had been trained over their lifetimes. I wondered how my daughters would see the world through their trained eyes.

You're Not Taking Command Seriously

May 2011—my wife and I were both students at Maxwell AFB's Air Command and Staff College (ACSC). We were about to embark on a career-long goal—squadron command. With the help of one of our mentors, we'd both been selected to do so on Kapaun Air Station, Germany, a little annex about three kilometers from Ramstein Air Base, a massive mobility hub for Europe.

We'd been waiting for this opportunity our whole career. Since we commissioned, it was ingrained in us that every officer worth their salt would command. We just needed to finish our academic studies so we could get back to the operational Air Force. To finish our one-year academic journey, I needed to complete one more seminar appropriately entitled, "Squadron Command."

Our task was simple, listen to briefings, read Colonel David Goldfein's book on Squadron Command, and develop our own leadership perspective, a five-minute presentation we could use at our first commander's call. I'd been mentored my whole career by some of the best commanders I'd ever seen. I'd also worked for terrible commanders and made note of what I did and didn't want to do. The task seemed pointless to me; I knew exactly how I was going to lead. Regrettably, I put forth the minimal effort in completing it. I was more worried about household goods pickup, change of command dates, and future German beer festivals.

We were asked to read our perspectives aloud to the class, then pair up with a seminar-mate to debrief one another. I read my perspective, a cocky, two-minute elevator speech lacking any real substance but with a great deal of hyperbole. I turned to my friend, callsign "Hooch," an F-15 Strike Eagle pilot and Weapons School grad, to debrief after class. Hooch was in my one-year elective and had traveled all over the world with me. He was someone I trusted, and I believed he knew who the real me was.

To my surprise, Hooch was bitterly disappointed with my effort. He told me I hadn't done a very good job and went on to say that I wasn't "taking command seriously." I was shocked; my jaw dropped open. I thought to myself, *Hooch, you know me! You know this is just academics and not the real world. I told you I learned from the best; I know exactly what I'm going to do when I take my flag—come on man!* But I bit my lip and simply said, "Thanks." I tucked his words into the back of my mind. I received my satisfactory grade and went on to graduate from ACSC with my wife. My family and I were off to Germany, a region we'd always dreamed of living in since we'd gotten married. I would never have guessed Hooch's words would come back to haunt me a few months later.

June 21, 2011—I took command of the 460th Space Communications Squadron, Detachment 1, a small unit of thirty active-duty, mostly first-term Airmen. Our communications mission was relatively easy but of national importance. It wasn't uncommon to receive a call from a three-star general when things weren't going smoothly. I believed this was going to be my finest hour; I just needed to do my part in leading this team of young Airmen.

In my mind, my leadership style was going to be very well-suited for this job. I took on the persona of a college head football coach. My alma mater, Auburn University, had just won the NCAA National Championship earlier that same year. Still riding that high, it was clear to me what my role was—I needed to get my Airmen qualified to do our unit's mission, and I needed to get them ready to perform at the next level, a large communications squadron, after they left my ranks. I got after this like any good coach would, through hours of practice. We ran checklists all day, again and again and again. I put forth nothing but positivity and motivational speech, what I'd seen from previous leaders that had worked in the past. Three months passed. My team quickly became proficient at our daily tasks, our communications uptime rates were excellent, and I treated the team with grilled bratwurst on the compound every Friday. With this overwhelming positivity and winning attitude, what could possibly go wrong?

It was 0930 on a Tuesday when I got a phone call. It was from the Base Defense Operations Center (BDOC) asking to speak to the unit commander. The Airman on the phone was calling to notify me that one of my Airmen had been taken into custody. The security forces had been called out to base housing early that morning due to a noise disturbance. When they had arrived at my Airman's house, they had found him heavily intoxicated and belligerent, many of his belongings destroyed, and his wife with what appeared to be a bruise forming on her face. Luckily, their two-month-old girl had been sound asleep. I was asked to come get him from the BDOC as soon as possible.

As I hung up the phone, I could feel the air being sucked out of my office. My stomach began to tighten into a knot, and I started to feel sick. My mind raced over what I needed to do in the next thirty minutes, the next hour, the next twenty-four hours. As I sat in my office in a daze, a stinging sensation shot down the back of my head. Hooch's words had come back to bite me because this was pretty damn serious, and I wasn't quite sure what to do.

After taking sage advice from my wife's First Sergeant, it was clear to me how I needed to proceed. I needed to separate my Airman from his wife and baby girl so I could ensure all parties were safe, then figure out what was going on. I needed to get the couple some help—base services that could give them counseling and hopefully heal this young couple. I needed to answer to my leadership chain. They would want to know how this happy-go-lucky commander would deal with his first taste of adversity. Lastly, I would need to hold my Airman accountable for not living up to the values of the Air Force and of our unit. So I did just that—I called my Airman into my office and told him he needed to stay at a courtesy room on Ramstein Air Base for a couple of nights, in effect removing him from his wife and child.

At first, this seemed a responsibility far beyond the scope of either a national championship football coach or a commander who saw himself as such. But if a player had acted without propriety, a football coach would simply suspend the player from the team. This Airman's family, his livelihood, was well within my scope of responsibility. It was my duty. And it is something I think about to this day.

Command is serious and should be treated as such. There's still a great deal of fun to be had but being deliberate in your preparation—keeping both the mission and the people in mind—is something I try to impart on every soon-to-be commander I meet.

Doug's Leadership Lessons

1. There are no one-size-fits-all solutions when dealing with human issues. There are policies, procedures, checklists, and mandates, but each human's situation is as unique as the origin stories of all the heroes in your unit. Sometimes you'll need to do the right thing rather than do things right.

2. No matter how well you've been groomed—the great bosses that have mentored you, the schools you've attended, the exclusive circles you're associated with—you will ultimately command as *yourself*. You can try to mimic what you perceive good leadership looks like, but your upbringing, values, and life experiences will shape how you lead and influence the decisions you make. Your values, and what you value, will become what your organization values.

3. Don't short-change the quiet ones, the ones who aren't nodding along with your ideas. Those members who do their jobs and are seldomly in the spotlight, what are they thinking about? Look at your table—is there anyone missing from it? Go seek out those voices and views. Concepts that may seem to be indisputable truths to you may have very different meanings to others. For me, the notion of "southern hospitality" may mean great things to many people, but I've seldom found that to be the case. I often wonder what other ideas I might have held true that those who worked for me did not.

DOUGLAS FREEMAN

Lt Col Douglas Freeman has served more than twenty-two years in the United States Air Force. The son of an Air Force Master Sergeant, Doug was raised in Montgomery, Alabama, and attended college at Auburn University, where he received his commission in 1998. Doug is married to Colonel Angela Freeman, and has served his entire career join-spouse in Hawaii, Germany, Illinois, Iraq, Turkey, and during several tours in the National Capital Region. Doug has had two successful command tours and has led teams at the agency, major command, and joint staff levels. He and Angela have two daughters, Helonna and Caria, who aspire to one day serve in the Air Force. Doug holds a B.S., a M.A., and a M.S.

When the Going Gets Tough...

by Doug W. Mabry

Commanding in COVID

I recall sitting with the Headquarters Air Mobility Command (HQ AMC) Commander's Battle Staff (CBS), listening to the HQ Chief of Staff brief the battle staff members on the latest COVID-19 updates. The CBS stood up to ensure the entirety of AMC had the necessary links to HQ resources twenty-four hours a day, enabling a rapid, efficient, and effective response to the pandemic. As a Squadron Commander on the HQ staff, this was not the first time I had represented the Intelligence Directorate (A2) at the CBS. We frequently supported the CBS for Combatant Command (COCOM) and Major Command (MAJCOM) level exercises, and in support of the Command's Humanitarian Assistance/Disaster Response (HA/DR) mission in response to several natural disasters around the globe.

However, there was something quite different about the feeling in the room during this meeting. For the first time, the enemy was not visible. Assessing this enemy's capabilities and possible intentions was not within the realm of possibility for even our most seasoned analysts. At that moment, the reality that the last four months of my command tour were going to look and feel drastically different than the first twenty months was beginning to settle in. From that moment forward, every single personnel decision I made was going to have a grave impact on the Airmen (Total Force) of the Air Intelligence Squadron (AIS). I'm not exaggerating when I say that due to the nature of the invisible enemy, some of those decisions were very much a matter of life or death. The quote from the Chief of Staff that night that would resonate with me throughout the following four months was this: "We are at *war* with this virus."

As HQ AMC began to implement social distancing policy to best protect the men and women of team Scott, I was soon told that we were authorized to bring just five percent of our workforce into work on any given day. Believe it or not, the easiest thing to do at that time was to work with the A2 and the other HQ AMC directorates to determine what we needed to "stop doing" due to the newfound resource constraints. For many years, we have worked under the belief that we would always be expected to do more with less. However, during this crisis, AMC leaders proved that we were simply expected to execute our highest priorities while deferring those that could be taken care of when we had additional manpower to rely on.

Of course, the tasks that did not require access to classified networks would continue as planned. However, what we soon discovered was that the Information Technology (IT) infrastructure was not prepared for that kind of workload. Although it was perfectly reasonable to still expect deadlines to be met, I learned a lot of lessons in applying a generous helping of grace to the many challenges my Airmen were facing. Prior to COVID-19, teleworking Airmen were expected to have the necessary tools and resources—an available workspace and a distraction-free environment—to meet their many work demands. The reality was that our Airmen were being sent to their homes to attempt to work while also struggling to access an overwhelmed Virtual Private Network (VPN) architecture and simultaneously taking on the role of schoolteacher. I knew my Airmen would never let the mission fail, so I had the luxury of focusing on the health and welfare of the men and women of the AIS.

From day one of my command tour, I espoused family values that I expected each member of the unit to adopt and adhere to. When I said family, I was sure to make it clear that I was not describing one of those dysfunctional families that never wanted to be around each other. I strongly desired that we would act like a family with genuine love, trust, and respect for one another. For twenty months, I felt this was one of the greatest aspects of the AIS, and the resiliency, care, compassion, and strength of my Airmen proved that to be true over the final four months. However, taking care of my family without the ability to see or interact with them on a daily basis was the greatest challenge of commanding in the COVID environment.

I truly loved seeing the smiling faces of our outstanding Airmen every single day. Now, if I was fortunate enough to be in the same room with them, we had to stay more than six feet apart and muffle our words through masks. Those interactions were sadly few and far between, and I was getting increasingly concerned about the mental and physical health of the AIS family. As each week passed and Airmen struggled with the travel and work restrictions placed on them, the overwhelming feeling of isolation became my gravest concern. I am eternally grateful for the strength and wisdom of my leadership team. I had a phenomenal Superintendent who deeply cared about every single member of the AIS family, a Director of

Operations who cared for the mission as deeply and passionately as he did the Airmen, and Division leaders who consistently displayed what it meant to selflessly care for the members of your military family. Despite the many IT challenges, they provided communication forums that kept the Airmen socially engaged and gainfully employed. I am also extremely thankful for the social networking tools like Microsoft Teams that allowed me to continue to execute Commander's calls and awards ceremonies, while still meeting all the Center for Disease Control (CDC)-recommended social distancing requirements.

I was deeply saddened that COVID denied me the opportunity to gather with the entirety of my AIS family one last time before handing the guidon over to my successor. Prior to COVID, we were planning a long-anticipated Combat Dining-In to serve as my going away party. Not only did I not get to see this plan come to pass, but there simply was no safe alternative. In addition, social distancing had to be maintained at the change of command ceremony. My final goodbye to the men and women I had dedicated my heart and soul to for two years had to be delivered over social media. Every single day, I wish the end of my command tour would have been quite different, but I count my many blessings that I did not lose any of my squadron family members to the deadly virus. I thank God for the strength and wisdom in the decisions I had to make, knowing now that every single Airman I brought to work had the daily potential of being exposed to this invisible enemy. Their lives were undoubtedly in my hands, but with God's grace, we not only survived, but continued to thrive.

My advice: When taking command, ensure that you immediately establish and cultivate a culture that you are confident will carry the organization through crises.

Losing a Loved One

I woke up on June 26, 2020 and immediately began reflecting on how quickly my command tour was coming to an end. It was beyond unfair that COVID-19 had stolen many precious moments from me and my AIS family in our last days together, but I couldn't help but reminisce on how amazing my tour had been and how blessed I was to serve the men and women of the greatest squadron on the planet. It was a Friday, meaning that I was going to have another opportunity to proudly wear my squadron colors beneath my Airmen Battle Uniform (ABU). However, this day was different. This was the *final* Friday prior to the change of command ceremony (the next Friday was part of the long Independence Day weekend), meaning this was the very last time that I would be sporting the AIS t-shirt in uniform.

Nothing extraordinary, or unusual, happened throughout the morning. In fact, my wife had already received the moving company at the house as this was less than two weeks out from my departure from Scott Air Force Base. The move was going smoothly, so I had the opportunity to continue preparations for the upcoming ceremony. It was just after 1300 when my office phone rang. It was the HQ AMC First Sergeant on the other end, and the words he uttered caused my heart to sink to the bottom of my stomach. He said, "Sir, I just got off the phone with Security Forces. Captain Nicholas Egich lost consciousness while swimming laps in the base pool. The lifeguards performed CPR on him at the side of the pool, and he is on his way to the Emergency Room now."

My mind was racing as it was completely unclear if he had already died or if the CPR was successful and he was going to pull through. I immediately briefed the Squadron Superintendent on what had happened and asked if he would be able to go with me to the hospital. As expected, he dropped everything to run out of the building with me. On our way out, we stopped to notify the AMC A2. When we reached my vehicle, it struck me that I did not have my government cell phone with me, and that I would need to stop by my house to pick it up. As I pulled up to the house, I immediately saw the moving company carrying my furniture out to the truck. In that very moment, I fully recognized that I was already leaning heavily on my wife to take care of the move for my family, and now there was a grave potential that I was going to be asking her to take on additional tasks if Nick was not going to survive this catastrophe. The truth is, she was more than ready for the moment at hand, and her actions, courage, and constant encouragement proved that I had nothing to be concerned about.

As I was leaving the house, my mind turned to the coming storm for Nick's wife and one-year-old child. I could hardly imagine the depth of pain they were about to endure, and I suddenly realized that she very well could have no idea that he was heading to the ER. He had gone to the base pool by himself, and clearly was not able to communicate his condition with her. The Superintendent and I stopped by the Egich home, and soon discovered that Mrs. Egich was already aware of her husband's condition and was on her way to the hospital. Although it was comforting for me to know that she had not been forgotten during the tragedy, I feared that she was not going to have the support she needed at the hospital when she received the worst news of her young life.

I arrived at the hospital shortly after departing Nick's house, and after a short delay in getting to the ER waiting room due to COVID protocols, the Superintendent and I finally made face-to-face contact with Mrs. Egich and the First Sergeant. When I asked if they had received an update on his condition, I witnessed the pain, disbelief, and shock in her eyes that I had feared as she informed me that he was gone. In that dark hour, I know that she had to be grateful to have her one-year-old daughter on her lap. She had no clue why her mommy was sad, and her sweet innocence warmed the hearts of everyone who had the privilege of watching her comfort a distraught human being in her greatest time of hurt.

As I talked with her about the great American and Airman and man that Nick was, we took some time to reminisce and share stories. While I struggled to find the right words to show compassion, empathy, and strength, my heart just wanted to find a place where I could cry and mourn the loss of my dear friend. However, the reality was that I could not be feeling anything close to the pain she was courageously suppressing. I realized that all my strength and energy needed to be focused on the surviving members of the Egich family, and on the men and women of the AIS family who were not yet aware of the loss of their beloved brother-in-arms.

As my Superintendent, the First Sergeant, and I continued to console and support Mrs. Egich to the best of our ability, we began to discuss the next steps we needed to take to ensure that all key leaders had been informed of Nick's death, in addition to the formal notification to our AIS family. One of the first of many exceedingly difficult decisions that needed to be made over a noticeably short timeframe was whether we should accept the health risks, considering all COVID protocols, of bringing all of the Squadron Airmen into a single location to make the formal notification. Knowing how hard the Airmen would take the catastrophic news, and their subsequent need to comfort each other in their time of grief, I saw no other reasonable option but to execute the recall and bring everyone to the base theater. The First Sergeant was instrumental in getting the necessary access, and our base services responded admirably to ensure temperature checks were conducted at the door as well as providing mental and spiritual wellness professional assistance.

I can still see the images of the socially distanced, mask-wearing crowd in my mind. I can also still hear the gasps, and sobs, from my AIS family members when I broke the news of Nick's passing. Once we were able to safely send all Airmen home for the night, my mind began to race as I considered everything that needed to be done over the next twelve days—ensuring we were continuing to take care of the Egich and AIS families, honoring the memory of Captain Nicholas Egich, and also preparing for the change of command. The next major decision that needed to be made was whether we would have the squadron memorial ceremony before my departure. I could not fathom handing over the guidon to the squadron without having the opportunity to celebrate Nick's life with my AIS family. I proposed that we should host the ceremony on July 7, 2020, the day prior to the change of command, and I am eternally grateful that the Egich family agreed and was willing and able to join us.

Throughout the entirety of my command tour, the AIS culture was to treat each other like a loving and respectful family. There were several moments throughout 2020 when that identity was put to the test, and I can proudly say that we came through those moments stronger each time. Little did I know that God would help us cultivate that culture in preparation for this crisis. There simply was no possible way to pull off back-to-back memorial and change of command ceremonies without the full dedication and commitment of every member of the AIS family. Every Airman was willing and ready to step into every role needed to ensure Nick was properly honored and the new Commander was appropriately welcomed because failure in either of those areas simply was not an option. Not a single day has passed that I have not thought about the pain my AIS family members have gone through. My heart aches at the thought of not being able to walk with them through the recovery process to the point of healing. However, I do sleep peacefully at night knowing that they have each other and that the family culture of the AIS will carry them through.

My advice: You will experience a high level of grief when suffering such a loss, but you must always remember that you are never alone as you lead your squadron family through it.

Doug's Leadership Lessons

1. Leadership/Command is a team sport.

2. Trust your leadership team to take care of *you*.

3. Take the time to truly *know* your Airmen.

DOUG W. MABRY

Lt Col Douglas W. Mabry is an instructor in the Leader Development Course (LDC) for Squadron Command. LDC's mission is "to inspire and equip air and space professionals to thrive on the command team." He previously served as the Commander of the Air Intelligence Squadron, Headquarters Air Mobility Command, Scott Air Force Base, Illinois. Doug entered the Air Force in 1998, and after serving four years as a member of the enlisted corps, he earned a commission in 2002 through Officer Training School, Maxwell Air Force Base, Alabama. He has deployed five times for contingency operations, most recently from October 2017 to April 2018 as the Deputy Director of Intelligence, Surveillance, and Reconnaissance (ISR) operations in support of Operation Resolute Support (ORS) in Afghanistan.

Investing in Connecting

by Jonathon "JB" Byrnes

Shortly after taking command of my second squadron in 2014, a tour that would last three years before all was said and done, I made a shrewd $200 investment in organizational effectiveness. That investment is bearing fruit, even today, for my successors in command. What kind of program that costs so little could have such a lasting impact on an organization of more than 500 personnel?

The American military has a long and storied history and an equally long and complicated relationship with alcohol use within the ranks. This has produced more than a few notorious episodes as use has crossed into abuse or good-natured fun has devolved into debauchery, but it also fuels the social interaction that has helped strengthen bonds and sow the seeds for strong friendships in times of strife that have later borne the fruits of victory. Many units have bars, though they are frequently referred to as heritage, training, or debriefing rooms to deflect unwanted attention from those who worry more about the negative impacts than the positive intent of such spaces. These spaces are used formally to gather and pass along news both good and bad, as well as to celebrate events such as promotions or retirements, and informally as places to connect with your comrades in arms.

First Contact—Observing the Market

During my first assignment, I was assigned to a flying squadron where I learned that while daily operations and meeting flying metrics were important, there was one event every officer made sure to schedule around—the Friday afternoon bar call. This was not because they desperately needed to drown their sorrows after a week of boldly going where no man had gone before; it was so they could get together with their fellow officers, unwind, and get to know each other better in a more relaxed setting. In fact, most of us lived several miles away from the base, so it was typically a single beer, or maybe just a can of soda so we would be safe to drive, but it was reassuring to know there was an opportunity to be together without having the daily grind of life in the office hanging around every corner.

I also witnessed that this wound up being a place to work through some tough conversations that were too sensitive to have during the normal duty day. This most often was related to buffoonery in the jet and was taken as an opportunity to level the bubbles between two comrades, but it could also be a chance to open up and ask for some help on a personal struggle or talk about career opportunities and how to navigate Air Force bureaucracy. As the most junior member, this left a lasting impression on me, seeing all ranks, from Lieutenant to Lieutenant Colonel (with occasional visits from the Colonels or the Brigadier General), relating, playing darts or dice, sharing a drink, and connecting as people.

What I witnessed every week was an exercise in emotional intelligence; watching as thirty to forty officers demonstrated varying degrees of self-awareness, self-management, social awareness, and relationship management. These four skills are what Bradberry and Greaves say constitute one's EQ, or emotional intelligence, and show how well people adapt and survive in groups. As a twenty-two-year-old Second Lieutenant in a room of seasoned officers, decades my senior in age and experience, I was nearly invisible. This gave me a front row seat to watch how to interact in the bar—what behavior was appropriate, who talked to whom, what conversations seemed the most difficult (and therefore the most valuable), and how each of them navigated the four quadrants of EQ. Some were more adept at self-awareness or self-management, quietly taking things in and adjusting their behavior discreetly. Others showed off their social awareness, smoothing things over, making introductions, or intervening in tense moments. And yet others clearly were masters of relationship management, taking the time to touch base with everyone in the room, having short yet meaningful conversations and then moving on to rekindle a lost conversation across the room.

Leadership Transition—Setting the Tone

I saw similar dynamics a few years later after moving to a Civil Engineer Squadron at a remote location. Here we would link up most days in the squadron bar after work. This was primarily because we all lived in dormitory rooms, and the bar acted as a living room for the squadron, open every night except Sunday. This bar was for all ranks, but to make that work, some oversight was required from the more senior folks in the squadron, and I volunteered along with about ten Senior Non-Commissioned Officers to make sure that everyone got back to their rooms safely and that should anyone be overserved, there would be somebody there to take care of them. In this setting, I was no longer the most junior attendee, and I often found myself the most senior, which changed my presence in the situation, but not the depth and quality of the interactions I saw happening and got to be a part of. The value of having leaders in the squadron routinely present in this environment was their accessibility to the Airmen and their demonstration that they were not just leaders who sat in an ivory tower, but people who could be related to one-on-one as friends.

As a leader in this situation, I was more cognizant of my self-management, controlling both my consumption as well as my tongue, not sharing sensitive information that my position exposed me to. I also practiced social awareness, knowing who was within earshot and, when necessary, guiding the conversation toward topics appropriate to the larger group. This was probably the best laboratory for relationship management, though, as I had to show that I could be open to having all the random untethered conversations that happen in a bar on any given night, take away a better understanding of the people I was having them with, and still be able to see them back on the job the next day without sacrificing the bonds we had built and while still maintaining my positional authority. Being present in the bar also allowed us as leaders to keep an eye on the mental health of the squadron. We could see whether there were rifts between people in a particular section, or if somebody was having a tough time adapting to being away from their family for a year, and intervene with either a kind ear or, when warranted, connecting them with resources to get them through that difficult time.

This made me practice being available and being myself while maintaining appropriate professional distance. I had seen many examples of how some leaders simply cite this professional distance as a reason for stepping back, shying away from more-than-surface-deep conversations, but I also saw that leaders who did remain distant weren't often the ones people came to when the going got tough, or when life was feeding them the proverbial shit sandwich. This showed me the value in creating deeper connections and going beyond superficial conversations to create the psychological safety people need from their leaders to trust them with tough problems.

Buying In—Friday Afternoon Mentoring

So what did I spend that $200 on? I handed it to my Chief, and I explained that I wanted him to pick up a variety of beverages (both alcoholic and non-alcoholic) to share with the squadron after my first Commander's Call at the end of the day that Friday. He and I talked about how we would execute this, what we had seen work before, what we had seen lead to problems, and how we could go about bringing the 500 people in our squadron together more as a family. We brought the other officers and Senior Non-Commissioned Officers (SNCOs) in on this plan and explained that as leaders in the squadron, we trusted them to assure we were all responsible for each other and for upholding standards. After I spoke for about thirty minutes that Friday, introducing myself to the squadron more in depth, I asked them to stick around and join me for a beverage. We had about fifty folks take me up on the offer. Some broke out tables to play dominos, others pressed a derelict dart board back into service, and we stayed for a couple of hours. I got to know my team, observe my leaders taking care of their people, and show the squadron that while I was in command, I would do my best to be accessible and available.

After that first week, the Chief, my Deputy, and I decided to make this opportunity a weekly event. I spoke to my boss, got approval to use my Squadron Training Room in this way, and let him know our plan. Each Friday, at least two of us would be available during the last thirty minutes of the duty day, beverages in hand, for any of the 500 people in the squadron to ask us questions and pick our brains, or for us to offer some mentoring. Over the course of my three years in command, unless I was off station for training or leave, I managed to make it to mentoring all but a handful of times, and those times, we had coverage from my Chief and Deputy as well as backup from our officers and SNCOs. This did not always mean that it was the end of my week, and I occasionally had to depart early for another meeting elsewhere on base, but by making it clear to my people that this was a priority to me and an opportunity I wanted them to take advantage of, it became routine to have thirty or more officers, enlisted personnel, and civilians turn up. I got to know much more about my people this way, and by being accessible like that, I was able to help explain the reasons behind some of the vexing policies we're occasionally asked to implement.

At the end of my command, as I reflected on what impact I'd had on the squadron, I realized that by creating the opportunity to interact, I had fostered a valuable forum to improve squadron performance by encouraging connections between people in different sections who would not normally interact to meet each other, learn a little more about them, and understand that they were part of the same big team and that you would be able to call them when you needed help with a tough problem. For me personally, it also created a place where I developed connections with people who would later need support both from me as well as the mental health community for personal crises.

Two of these were military members, one who suffered from extreme combat related post-traumatic stress, and the other who had fallen into extreme depression following both personal and work-related setbacks. The relationships I had with them created a willingness in both to tell me that they were struggling more than they had let on, that they had thoughts of hurting themselves, and that they were not sure that they could keep fighting their personal demons. That directness then let my leadership team connect them with mental health professionals who ultimately brought them both in for long-term residential treatment. From this, one of them returned to duty and was promoted a few years later, continuing to serve while receiving treatment. The other medically retired and has been continuing treatment as he moves on to the next chapter in his career. Had I not spent the time getting to know these two personally in the bar over a beer, making the effort to understand what they were going through, I do not think they would have confided in me the way they did when they needed real help. This validated my decision to drink at work, to stretch my EQ legs, and to let my people connect to me as a person.

Bringing it Home—Paying Attention to What Matters Most

On February 14, 2016, I received a Letter of Admonishment. I had been in command at RAF Lakenheath for nearly twenty-one months of what would in the end be a thirty-seven-month command tour, and things had been going great. The squadron was firing on all cylinders with more than 600 motivated Liberty Engineers leading the way and making every other organization on base successful in their missions. Where had I gone wrong? Was this something I could recover from? What was I missing?

As I reflected on this, I thought back to my previous command tour, which I had crushed, and I tried to figure out where I had gone astray; where was this blind spot that had allowed me to jerk the wheel and get rear-ended?

When I was teaching the Leader Development Course for Squadron Command (LDC), the first morning we talked about Culture and Cognitive Diversity. As an engineer, those were things that I had seen make a difference, and I have been able to analyze them enough to get behind them as ideas. The next topic we talked about was personality through the lens of 16Personalities, Myers-Briggs, Personality Types, and Emotional Intelligence, something that I never could understand and had always just blown off because where are the facts? What data proves this is real? Well, once I joined the LDC team, I got to see some of the practical applications behind these theories, but more importantly I had a chance to reflect on my career, and now I see that if I had paid attention to this stuff when I was exposed to it, I could have been a better leader, mentor, and Wingman, and might have avoided that LOA. So what is it that finally made it click for me? How did LDC overcome my years of training and practice as an engineer?

Let me take you back to September 2011. I had just deployed to the 405th Expeditionary Civil Engineer Squadron, Thumrait Air Base, Oman, as the Commander. Leading up to that leadership laboratory, I had exactly *zero* days of pre-command training, but I was an Ops Chief at Joint Base McGuire-Dix-Lakehurst, and I had been commissioned for twelve years, so *game on!*

As I went through that deployment, I was surrounded by a great team who was able to get things done with amazing speed, focus, and efficacy. They did all I asked and more, and they continually swept the monthly Group awards. I was extremely lucky.

At the end of the deployment, my boss, Col Dave Knight, a crusty old Herc Nav, sat me down and gave me my final feedback. What I heard was that I was a great Civil Engineer who had a great team behind me and that he appreciated the ECES's ability to make his vision a reality. He gave me my Letter of Evaluation (LOE), and I was ranked his number one of five Squadron Commanders ahead of four Lieutenant Colonels, all of whom were sitting or graduated Squadron Commanders at home station. I left feeling great about myself and my team and looking forward to getting back home.

Now over the next eight years, I told my war stories and had other great successes and more opportunities to lead. But something I have always struggled with was how to mentor my CGOs, SNCOs, and Senior Civilians in a way that could help them be better Airmen, Wingmen, and Warrior Leaders. So I spent my time teaching them all how to better use the tools from their CE training, sharpening those blades, because that's what I had taken from Col Knight's feedback, but that never seemed to translate into making them better leaders.

Fast-forward to February 2019, just down the hall in Seminar 3, when I once again was being taught personality types. Now, granted, I had already been hired to be an instructor in this course, so I had to keep my eye-rolling and direct challenging of the material through sarcasm in check, lest I be voted off the island before I PCSed (permanent change in station, which means moving) up here. So I let down my guard and leaned in, trying to find something that would let me grab on and say, "I can teach this with a straight face." And I got to thinking, what is it that let me succeed throughout my Air Force Career? How was I able to wash out of Pilot Training and a mere ten years later find myself sitting in Oman, commanding 113 Airmen, or two years after that in England, leading over 600? And I thought back to that feedback from Col Dave Knight and what it was he was really telling me. What had made me his number one Squadron Commander? Not a single part of that feedback had anything to do with me being a great Civil Engineer, but everything to do with me knowing myself.

His feedback was:

1. You are comfortable and confident out in front of a meeting or a formation—you prefer extraversion to introversion when you interact with people.

2. You have an operational mindset; you see the big picture,

then make the details fit—you prefer intuition to sensing in my data collection.

3. You make decisions that are best for the whole group somehow without alienating those who do not get their way—you prefer feeling over thinking when making decisions.

4. You are able to adjust on the fly to new info and are open to all options—you prefer perceiving over judging when getting to work.

Now some of that probably sounds pretty touchy-feely and unscientific, probably why my engineer brain never latched on, but hopefully these stories can help you learn a new vocabulary and a new way to think about who you are, to know yourself.

So how did I go from the number one of five Squadron Commanders in the 405th Air Expeditionary Group to less than four years later holding a Letter of Admonishment addressed to me from my boss?

The LOA was handwritten and only really had two sentences of substance. It read, "Looking forward to reconnecting. I miss you."

The boss I'd gotten from is also the mother of my children, my best friend, and my partner in life. I have known Sheri since I was twelve years old—started dating her when I was fifteen—and we have been together ever since. We have two kids, five college degrees, twelve PCSs, three deployments, three short tours, and nearly ten years geographically separated from each other over the last twenty-six years together. In February 2016, Sheri had just finished her dissertation defense and been awarded her Ph.D., so what I took from her note at the time was she was now ready to spend more time on us since she was done with that significant undertaking.

Like any good engineer, I took that input as her saying she was going to refocus. I was doing great, but now that her calendar was a lot clearer, we were going to be heading for new heights together. I diverted some attention away from the office, we took better advantage of being in Europe by taking more family trips, and I kept my focus on command. The next sixteen months flew by, minor course corrections came in from Sheri when I was too focused on work, but nothing major. Everything was fine.

We finished strong at Lakenheath. I was dual-tasked as the Deputy 48th Mission Support Group Commander the last eight months of my command. Life was busy, but we were still making time to travel, the kids were doing well, Sheri was working and using her new degree, and the squadron was doing even better than it had been in 2016.

We PCSed to Southern Command, living in Miami, Florida, restoring our Vitamin D, and enjoying the convenience of life in America again. The new job was far less demanding of my time, so Sheri and I were able to hang out more together one-on-one. Everything was fine.

In December 2018, we found out I'd been selected for Air War College. We had a long discussion about what was best for the family, kids, high school timing for our son, us, and what things might look like if I went to Maxwell AFB alone. We also considered what we would do if I then got a remote out of War College, keeping in mind that the following year, the odds of a deployed command would be pretty high too. So we decided that we were better parents as a team and that we needed to keep the family together as much as the Air Force would allow us to within our own control. That decision was reinforced when the opportunity to become an LDC instructor was presented. We knew that the two-year option would at least delay any possibility of deployment until after Andrew, our oldest, had graduated from high school. And I would get to teach leaders how I crushed my time in command—a win-win.

In February 2019, I went to Maxwell to meet the LDC team and learn about the curriculum. This personality type/human domain stuff can really make people better leaders, officers, mentors, Commanders, etc.

After being in Alabama for a few months, I found that card from Sheri while cleaning out boxes from our move from Florida. I re-read it and reflected on it through my improved knowledge of myself, and I realized what I was actually being told by my most trusted advisor. I felt the gut punch I should have felt when she'd delivered it three years ago. I found my blind spot. Sheri was asking me to use those considerable skills that Col Knight had lauded me for and that my time at Lakenheath had reinforced, to actually reconnect. I was the one who hadn't been present in the way she needed. I'd been a moron.

Fortunately, Sheri is a nurse, and has far more patience with me than I deserve, so there isn't a broader cautionary tale for me to relay today, but I am rethinking, relearning, rebuilding, and reconnecting every day now. Not just with Sheri, but also with Andrew and Allison, our little minions. Using the framework and the vocabulary I'd learned for LDC, I now have blind spot radar.

I also now see that what had allowed me to succeed as an Air Force Civil Engineer had not been my skill as an engineer, a designer, or constructor (frankly, I'd gotten C's in most of my design courses at the Academy), but my ability to build teams that could work together and communicate more effectively.

As you finish reading this chapter, I challenge you to open your mind to this stuff, reflect on leaders you have both admired and dreaded seeing at work, and think about who you are and how you can be a better Airman, Wingman, partner, spouse, parent, or leader. Spring for the blind spot radar. It makes driving a whole lot easier.

If you have the opportunity to lead an organization, I

recommend finding effective ways to connect with your team. First, understand the culture by observing the market. Then decide how you want to deliberately take part by setting the tone as a leader. Figure out the right avenue through which to connect and buy in by prioritizing the event on your calendar and consistently making the effort to use it. And lastly, turn on your blind spot radar by paying attention to what truly matters most by bringing those skills and your focus home with you too.

As I move into new jobs, I will be thinking deliberately about these lessons and how to be there for my people.

JB's Leadership Lessons

1. When you are a leader in an organization, find an effective way to connect with your team. First, understand the culture by observing the market and seeing what is already available and working that you might capitalize on.

2. Then decide how you want to deliberately take part, to set the tone as a leader. The value of having leaders routinely present in a relaxed environment, accessible to their people, and demonstrating that they are not just leaders who sit in an ivory tower, but people who can be related to one-on-one as friends.

3. Once you find the right avenue for connection that fits your organization, buy in by prioritizing the event on your calendar and consistently making the effort to be present, be engaged, and be using that opportunity to connect.

JONATHON "JB" BYRNES

Colonel Jonathon "JB" Byrnes has spent twenty-two years as a leader in a variety of flying and civil engineering organizations. As a leader, he strives to always be available to listen, does his best to see problems from all sides, and loves working with a team to solve wicked problems with novel solutions that others miss. He is eagerly awaiting opportunities to help the Air Force reinvigorate how they provide installation and mission support as an enterprise and commanding and leading at the next level. JB holds a B.S. in Civil Engineering, a M.S. in Construction, and a Master of Strategic Studies.

Clarity of Purpose

by Jeremy M. "JP" Ponn

Show Them the Forest

One of the most important things to understand for the Soldiers, Sailors, Marines, Airmen, and Guardians that serve with us is their unique contribution to the mission. Without that understanding, that clarity of purpose, ownership, performance, and morale suffer. I wrote the story below one dreary evening at Ramstein Air Base as I awaited the return of one of the highest-profile missions my unit was tasked with during my tenure.

Just before 1 a.m. (7 p.m. EDT) on Saturday, Oct. 13, a Ramstein-assigned C-37 delivered Andrew Brunson to his first stop on a return trip to the United States. Brunson, a U.S. pastor who lived and ministered in Turkey, had been held by the Turkish judiciary for two years following the attempted coup in 2016.

The White House-directed mission, executed on short

notice just hours after initial notification, flawlessly demonstrated the 86th Airlift Wing's ability to provide professional
airlift to any country, any time, from the pavement up. Most
importantly, it showcased that our airlift mission was truly a
team sport.

All too often, we collectively get lost in the daily grind of
our day-to-day mission, and as the adage goes, it is hard to see
the forest for the trees. While I'm sure this summary may omit
an outstanding contributor to the incredibly talented team that
made this mission happen, allow me to highlight a few ways in
which Ramstein Airmen touched our ability to repatriate Pastor
Brunson.

The notification began at 1:01 a.m. via telephones and
networks maintained by 86th Communications Squadron
personnel. Initially, details were sparse and required the
transfer of original tasking discussions to secure internet
protocol network traffic—another 86th CS touchpoint. As
details unfolded, members of a 76th Airlift Squadron crew
who were scheduled to complete a local training sortie were
reassigned to support the mission. As initial details of the
pickup location were passed to the 86th Operations Group,
86th Logistics Readiness Squadron fuels personnel were
alerted to increase the fuel load on the aircraft to allow the
crew to fly to and from Turkey without the need to refuel on the
ground, expediting Pastor Brunson's return.

Members of the 86th Aeromedical Evacuation Squadron
and the 86th Medical Group prepared to provide Pastor
Brunson with medical care, to include the last-minute addition
of a flight surgeon and nurse to the growing crew from the 76th
AS. The 86th Operations Support Squadron provided time-
sensitive intelligence and facilitated the arming of aircrew

members who were flying into an unknown political situation. 76th AS flight attendants quickly rushed to the DECA Commissary to shop and prep Pastor Brunson's first meal on American "soil"—the C-37 aircraft. Commissary personnel opened dedicated lanes to allow the crew to quickly check out and move on to preparing meals for Pastor Brunson and his wife.

The crew was supported by a host of entities in the 86th OG who professionally worked diplomatic clearance issues with 86th OSS and 603rd Air Mobility Division personnel. The crew stepped to the jet and prepared to launch off airfield surfaces maintained by 86th Civil Engineer Group personnel. Simultaneously, another crew was placed in crew rest to transfer Pastor Brunson back to the U.S. after a planned short refueling stop (86th LRS again) and crew change, facilitated by transient alert contract personnel.

As is often the case with short notice missions, things changed. Plans were adjusted for a possible stay of a few days at Landstuhl Regional Medical Center, supported by 86th MDG personnel and a joint force of caregivers just up the hill. Ultimately, the decision was made to execute a short overnight stay, enabled by Force Support Squadron personnel and the 86th AW Protocol office. 86th Security Forces defenders secured the ramp and provided escort for U.S. State Department personnel who arrived from all over Germany to welcome Pastor Brunson. 86th OSS personnel safely and efficiently guided the aircraft to an approach at Ramstein in the dead of night with fog rolling onto the airfield using instrument landing systems maintained by their personnel and powered by the 86th CEG. Again, the 86th LRS had touched the mission, providing transportation for Pastor Brunson and his wife from the flight line to the hotel in a bus professionally maintained by 86th

Vehicle Readiness Squadron personnel.

Overnight, while Pastor Brunson slept, members of the 86th Maintenance Group completed inspections on the jet, preparing it for the alert crew the next morning. That crew, unable to prepare the 76th AS's standard of exemplary service while in alert status, were helped by a host of additional 76th AS personnel who prepped food for the next day's mission. At 5:45 a.m. the next morning, the crew was alerted while Pastor Brunson was provided medical care by the 86th MDG. The jet departed at 9:11 a.m. arriving exactly on time at 12 p.m. EDT at Andrews Air Force Base, Md., where Pastor Brunson was greeted by members of the State Department and rushed to a meeting with President Donald Trump just two hours later.

So if you ever wonder how you contribute to the 86th Airlift Wing's mission of Professional Airlift, remember this story. It takes a team, and the members of the 76th AS and I salute your support and dedication to our mission. Each one of you plays a part every day; remember that the next time you're looking at that task you do each day—they all matter. This entire team makes Professional Airlift happen.

This was my attempt to let *every* Airman on Ramstein know what part they played in making this, and every, mission a success. Share your success with your fellow brothers and sisters in arms. That simple act will go much further than you can imagine.

Family

What about sharing that clarity of purpose beyond the "walls" that bound the military members in your organization? The Air Force has a saying, and I'd imagine that the other services have a similar one: "We recruit Airmen, but we retain families." While COVID-19 economic impacts have resulted in excellent retention for the time being, I believe that retaining our best and brightest will remain a priority for every service as opportunities in the civilian sector return to pre-pandemic levels.

When I arrived at the 76th Airlift Squadron at Ramstein Air Base in the summer of 2016, I was beyond excited to return to a squadron family after spending the last several years working staff in the Pentagon. To my surprise, I found a loose collection of several small groups that were getting the job done and doing it well but lacked an identity and sense of cohesion. While we had some success closing the gaps while I was the Operations Officer, I made strengthening the 76th family one of my top two initial priorities when I took the guidon a few years later. Overseas, that shared identity and support system isn't just a nice-to-have, it is an imperative in my mind. My wife and I made sure that the feeling of family extended to every member of our Airmen's families as well if they wished to participate.

We made it a point to be at every flight that landed with new family members for our squadron, every available member in tow, just to make sure our new members *and* their families felt welcome. This policy made a lasting impact for each new family. Instead of wondering where to go as they stumbled in a sleep-deprived state off a trans-oceanic flight, they were met with a sea of smiling faces. It was a happy start and first impression for their new home away from home.

That said, not all the moments I shared with the spouses were happy ones. Two events that required deliberate communication of the importance of our mission with the spouses of my members come to mind immediately. The obvious one that I'm sure you're thinking of was the COVID-19 response, but the second proved to be a little more tense for our families due to the short notice that preceded it.

Following the U.S. airstrike that killed General Qasem Soleimani on January 3, 2020, and the subsequent response and unrest that unfolded in the region and across the Levant, we elevated our posture in the squadron to be prepared to respond to time-critical airlift in any manner that may be required. As a result of that posture, all leave and passes were cancelled and travel by military members was restricted to mission-critical temporary duty only. The military members understood the situation that could escalate rapidly through several proxy forces in the region, but I felt it crucial to explain our new posture to the spouses of the unit as well. I was upending plans in their lives and they needed to know why, directly from the horse's mouth.

My wife and I hosted a meeting for all spouses, leaning on the spouses of the unit that had been through this kind of event before to help the younger spouses through this uncertain time. While most of the spouses knew what their members did each day, I needed to give them more context, to provide clarity of purpose for our mission. I provided some unclassified context to the operational plans that our unit supported, and why it was so critically important that we were prepared to support them at a moment's notice. Lives may very well have been at stake. The more "seasoned" spouses did an excellent job supporting the more than forty percent of spouses who were experiencing this uncertainty for the first time. It was a wild success—spouses had buy-in for the mission, they knew why recent restrictions had been put in place, and they rallied behind their members to support the mission.

When COVID-19 struck the European continent in early March that same year, I again had some hard decisions to make, and more importantly, to communicate. Due to the size of my unit, and the probability of being called on to execute time-sensitive operational support airlift of medical supplies and testing materials, I again instituted limitations on my Airmen. While the DoD had already released travel restrictions, I jumped ahead of the Wing in how I implemented those restrictions and telework policies due to my finite numbers of mission-critical crew force.

Again, the communication campaign was critical, and it could not be only directed at the military members. The entire family had to know the why—my priority was to protect my members and their families *and* to preserve combat capability for United States European Command. While social distancing precluded face-to-face meetings with the spouses, we utilized a litany of electronic methods to make sure they were receiving the support they needed and information about the critical mission that their spouses were about to embark on. We would get the call; it was just a matter of when. My message to the squadron scarcely two weeks later is below:

Doves,

It's time. I hope you all have enjoyed this break with your families because we're about to get to work. The entire reason we've been preserving combat capability is just around the corner.

In coming days, we'll be called on to execute missions that may be more important than any that you have ever flown. We won't be carrying generals to end wars. We won't be repatriating pastors after years of prison.

You'll be carrying the tools to wage war with an enemy that has silently come to battle the entirety of humanity. As of now, you can expect regular set schedules that fly to the same locations every other day on both of our aircraft. We'll be distributing PPE supplies, test kits, and anything else needed throughout the theater and returning some items for local processing. These routes will continue until no longer needed, so buckle down and get ready to work.

We are not planning on passengers at this time. While the risk of exposure is low in that regard, be vigilant while executing this crucial mission. You will be interacting with ground crews and delivery personnel. Limit interactions and distance yourselves. Practice good hygiene on any surface that can introduce risk to you and your fellow aviators, and we'll pop out on the other side of this battle just fine.

"To each there comes in their lifetime a special moment when they are figuratively tapped on the shoulder and offered the chance to do a very special thing, unique to them and fitted to their talents. What a tragedy if that moment finds them unprepared or unqualified for that which could have been their finest hour."

—Winston Churchill

Now is your "tap on the shoulder" moment. You are all more than prepared and qualified to execute this mission that is unique to your talents. Let's add another proud line to our Dove heritage.

—JP

Make sure your Soldiers, Sailors, Marines, Airmen, and Guardians understand the "why." Return to it frequently so that they connect themselves to the big picture. Don't let the day-to-day blur their purpose. Once you have done that and established a method to return to this message frequently, share that same message with their families in as many venues as possible.

JP's Leadership Lessons

1. *One cool judgement is worth a thousand hasty counsels.*
– President Woodrow Wilson, January 29, 1916

2. Train your replacement. Find someone that you can help become a better version of you and help them achieve *their* version of greatness.

3. Build and keep your family strong. Treasure each member from all your "families," and treat them how they want to be treated.

JEREMY M. "JP" PONN

Colonel Ponn is a devoted husband, father of three young women, and caretaker to three fur babies. He is a USAF mobility pilot with flight time in the C-21A, C-17A, KC-135, C-37A, and C-40B aircraft. He commanded the 76th Airlift Squadron at Ramstein AB, Germany, prior to his assignment at Air University. His focus while in command was developing a sense of family for his entire unit—a task that is never finished, but beyond fulfilling in the endeavor.

To Lead

by William J. "JW" Watkins

I Can't Say I'm a Winner

This isn't a story about how awesome I am, how great a leader I am, or even how I did this awesome thing, took that hill, led my team to greatness, etc. This isn't about that. This is a short story about one man's early journey navigating life and organizational challenges, self-doubt, shifting priorities, and, well, luck that ultimately did lead to helping others.

And yet, I have succeeded. "Made it?" Probably not, but who cares? I'd like to think I made a difference in the lives I had responsibly over during my moment as a Commander. That matters to me, and I hope it mattered to them. And so, as a lifelong service-member (25.5 years and counting in the United States Air Force), I've witnessed a thing or two—defining moments—that test one's staying power. Notice I didn't say character. This isn't about that either. It's more a story of adapting and learning.

I enlisted in the Air Force in '95 amid the backdrop of my own dysfunctional family issues. My dad and I hadn't spoken in a year. I lived on my own my senior year of high school. I was on food stamps, and had gotten myself emancipated, a long, boring story of teenage defiance. I enlisted to piss him off. Turns out that idea hadn't worked either.

And so, there I was, one month after I turned eighteen, at Lackland AFB, Texas. In June. Hot as hell. I think it was the hottest place on Earth I'd ever experienced. Let me tell you, when I got there, I had something to prove. I really didn't care about the games they made us play in Basic Military Training. My motivation was to prove to my dad I could be awesome at something despite his disapproval. So my motivation was spite. And as a result, my start in the Air Force was, well, rocky.

My first mistake was using the B-word to describe my military training instructor (TI) to some random recruit standing next in line for chow, whom I had just met on day two, and my TI, an athletic but short, fiery female TSgt, overheard the derogatory expletive. Let me tell you, that did not go well for me. I remember her to this day putting her finger on my nose, backing me against the wall, and shouting/spitting every obscenity she could muster. She completely lost it, and I deserved it. I was an unruly teenager, joining the Air Force completely out of spite, and had a lot to learn. She made me her "house mouse." Basically, I had to clean her room in addition to my personal bunk space, and she went out of her way to make it extra dirty. I eventually survived that, but my hopes to earn BMT honor graduate? Dashed. She made sure of it.

When I got to tech school to learn how to become a "weapons troop," my attitude had dramatically changed. I barreled down even harder. Having failed at showing my dad how awesome I could be in basic, I was focused more than ever on proving myself again. One thing I'm thankful for in the Air Force is that I've been given opportunity after opportunity to mess up and grow.

So, in tech school, while my older peers were looking for every opportunity to socialize, party, or whatever, I studied. And studied. And learned to study some more. I received a perfect score on eleven out of fourteen blocks of academic instruction. I seriously never left my room. I lived off $20 per week. I exercised, watched what I ate, really boring stuff, but I was so motivated to prove myself. Living off $20 a week was no big deal for me, all things considered, seeing as how I'd been on food stamps just a few months earlier. Anyway, the commandant said I had the highest academic average they'd ever seen, and yeah, finally something I could take to Pops.

Speaking of which, we started talking again. He didn't ask about my work or achievements, so you know what? I didn't tell him. That bothered me and motivated me still. When I got to my first squadron at Shady J, NC, I thought I'd made it. Boy, was I wrong. Here is where I met the first of two people who absolutely changed me, influenced me, and shaped me foundationally.

MSgt Joe Jackson

The 335th Fighter Squadron Weapons Section Superintendent. I was scared of him. He was a big guy. He would line up the entire section every Monday and talk to every young Airman in the flight. He had something to say to every single one of us. This was my first exposure to luck, because if it weren't for MSgt Jackson, I wouldn't be here today. You see, he saw right through me. He knew I needed to be challenged. He connected with every single person who graced his presence. I never once saw him lose his cool, ever. And trust me, with a flight of around 100 weapons troops, we gave him plenty of reasons to lose his cool. He drove home a value of excellence that I had never seen before. He challenged me to think every time we spoke. So I gave him my all, finished my upgrade training in record fashion, rocked my test scores, and got promoted "below the zone" to Senior Airman. I'll never forget his words of encouragement to this day. "Jason, what do *you* want to be in the Air Force? A General? Because you sure are working on it!"

So, my first "skill" you could say I developed was the skill to connect. I didn't realize it at the time, but that was perhaps the most useful leadership tool imparted unto me, to this day. I still write Reverend Jackson (he's a Pastor now), and he still writes me.

Fast-forward to my second assignment in Anchorage, Alaska. I had met the love of my life, had gotten married, and was taking evening classes at the local college. I made Staff Sergeant my first attempt testing. So luck had struck again. This time, my mentor was a TSgt by the name of Steve Jones. Steve was an organized perfectionist. Turns out he was a mentee to MSgt Jackson, as well, years back. Small Air Force. Like Sgt Jackson, Steve never lost his cool. Steve was the epitome of strong servant leadership. He absolutely poured his heart and soul into developing Airmen, and I was lucky enough to be that guy. He pushed me toward new challenges, carefully guiding from the sidelines. He set me up. I was going to get out of the Air Force, but he helped get me into a commissioning program where I could pursue my passion for school full-time while retaining my pay. I would not be where I am today without his input into my life either. He shaped me, cultivated me. So the next key trait that is fundamental to who I am is my belief that one should cultivate their people—look for, develop, and find ways to help them grow.

I went off to Officer Training School eventually, thanks to an application that Steve helped me put together, by the way. Things were good for a while. I repaired my relationship with my dad, my wife and I had our first baby on the way, I got selected for the aircraft

I wanted to fly, the F-15E, as a Weapon Systems Officer, and I finished as the top grad during my F-15E basic course training (all due to the study habits and work ethic I had learned as a young Airman).

But at my first base as an operational flyer, I faced a new set of challenges that once again required a different level of adaptation. Except this time, I was on my own. I didn't have a Joe Jackson or Steve Jones in my corner. And it showed. For the first time since high school, I was exposed to a culture of utter dysfunction compared to my earlier military experiences, characterized by dog-eat-dog competition, people stepping over each other, narcissism, bullying, and all topped off by the infamous boogeyman we all know of by now—toxic leadership. Yes, all of those bundled up into one assignment. I loved Alaska, and I loved flying, but my new hostile environment rubbed off on me in so many ways that it nearly cost me my marriage.

I was stressed, I gained weight, and I started to lose my way. No one cared. My colleagues were leaving the Air Force in droves. My first supervisor was busted for cocaine usage. Our weapons officer, the esteemed "look-up-to" flyer in our organization, drove a supercilious "us vs. them" culture with the younger flyers. You were either part of the "in" crowd, or you were worthless. For example, I was so convinced that as a young Fighter Squadron LT I had to be at every squadron "roll call" that I almost missed the birth of my second child. The fear and reality of ridicule were pervasive. My first commander, absent, never said more than two or three words to me that I can truthfully remember. He was an elitist, and he ran an elitist culture. I wondered, how had I left the "lowly" enlisted ranks, where I'd been challenged and supported, only to be left with this as an officer in the Air Force that I loved? I wanted out.

But as luck would have it, I moved. Another opportunity. This time to Idaho, and with that, new leadership. With the change of one commander, everything changed. This guy, who went by "Tex," cared about people. He didn't just talk the talk, he knew our culture had problems, and he went out of his way to adjust. Friday afternoons, when the additional duties were traditionally accomplished in a Fighter Squadron, followed by culturally mandated aircrew meetings *starting* at 1630, followed by weapons talk and then roll calls that could go on until late in the night, he canceled them. While I was the Fighter Squadron Chief of Scheduling, he would walk into my office around 1000 every Friday and ask me to adjust the schedule to get everyone out of the building by 1400. His focus? Family and quality of life. He gave us time, time that mattered. Not a single fighter squadron commander had communicated that up to that point in my career. He made us realize what was important. He communicated his values, his intent, and he made sure we all knew it.

So my final key lesson I've learned, fundamental to who I have become, is on the value of communication. Communicate what's important. Speak to people in their preferred medium, at their level, and most importantly, listen. Listen not just to individuals, but to the group. Communication ties directly into the other two components of my style, connection and cultivation. These three ideas, connection, cultivation, and communication, form the basis of how I lead today, my personal leadership triad. That's what I think makes one effective.

Effective at what, you ask? Well, that's the rub. To me, what makes my organization, the Air Force, the best of its type in the world, isn't the technology, the bright shiny objects, or the tactics we employ; rather, it's the people, or more precisely, their ability to grow stronger by teaching, creating, and molding their replacements. That's what Steve Jones, Joe Jackson, and Tex Coe imparted on me. To grow people in any capacity, you have to connect with them, and in order to connect with them, you have to communicate what's important, and you have to know how to communicate with them. You need all three of these traits to effectively grow and motivate— to lead, in my opinion. They depend on each other, and they are inextricably linked. At year twenty-three, I took command of the largest Operations Support Squadron in Europe. It was an awesome and utterly amazing experience. I built my culture on my philosophical leadership triad. I beat the message over and over. I like to think it hit home with a few people.

I may have had silver oak leaves on my shoulder, but that MSgt wisdom imparted on me some twenty-three years earlier still stuck with me. In fact, I wrote a personal letter to the parents of one of my deployed Airmen, a SSgt Survival Evasion Resistance and Escape (SERE) specialist who was having a difficult time being away from his young family over Christmas, and his mother wrote me back and reached out to her deployed son too. It was just the message he needed at the right time to give him a little boost. When he returned from combat, he marched right into my office and gave me a big hug. Our connection strengthened into an unbreakable trust, and he went on to lead his SERE section boldly, earning himself a rare Stripes for Exceptional Performers promotion to Technical Sergeant from the base commander.

Then, coming full-circle, I got to give back a little of what TSgt Jones had done for me. Before I closed out my command, I wrote two Officer Training School recommendations for two of my NCOs, both of whom were selected to trade stripes for bars. Since leaving, I've written three letters of recommendation, and watched several of my Airmen go on to greatness. And also, thanks to leaders like Tex, I learned not only to talk the talk, but to walk the walk as a commander. I communicated what I valued, but most importantly, I learned that communication starts with listening to the needs, hopes, wants, and desires of one's Airmen and their families. I prioritized a resource that, once spent, is forever gone: time. When the mission was complete, we closed shop, sending people home to their families. In the end, I sincerely hope I had a role in saving an "Airman Watkins" or two in my unit, like the way I was guided and redirected at foundational points in my career. I guess I will never know for sure, but whatever impact I had, it's because of the few good leaders who invested in me and my life.

JW's Leadership Lessons

1. Leadership is the courage to inspire and develop someone else; it is not defined by title or rank.

2. To effectively inspire and develop someone else, you need to connect with them effectively. This is an act of curiosity and love that builds trust.

3. So now we have trust—but so what? It is incumbent on the leader to do something with it, to cultivate someone else's potential into what they desire to be.

WILLIAM J. "JW" WATKINS

Lt Col W. Jason Watkins is currently an instructor at the Chief of Staff of the Air Force's Leader Development Course for Squadron Command. He is an experienced F-15E Weapon Systems Officer with seven operational deployments. Previously, he commanded the 48th Operations Support Squadron at RAF Lakenheath, UK. He is a husband, father, friend, coach, avid intramural sports player, and perpetually curious about what makes people around him happy. JWat has several degrees including an M.P.A. and M.Sc.

Journeys of Forgiveness, Gratitude, and Courage in Love, Loss, and Leadership

by John M. Hinck, PhD

My Family's Journey

On October 20, 1944, General Douglas MacArthur and his forces landed in the Philippines and fulfilled his promise of "I shall return." A few days later, American forces began liberating the many POW camps near Manila. Among the survivors were six Hincks: my grandmother and family patriarch, Dorothy; my father, Ed; my aunts, Ethel and Mary Lou; and two uncles, John and Robert. After almost three years of being held captive by Japanese forces, the surviving family members boarded boats and began their new journeys. Upon arrival in San Francisco, they decided to move to Fresno due to incredibly good housing offered to POWs and internees. I remember growing up surrounded by family and extended family.

My father's family rarely talked about their final years on the islands, but when they did, it always centered on how their time as prisoners had made them take nothing for granted. They had little notice they would be captured, and no idea that the internment would last more than three years (my father was a POW from age eighteen to twenty-one). Lack of food deteriorated their health; after his experience, my father would eat everything on his plate, wasting nothing.

My family lost parents and friends in WWII; therefore, they spent much time together because their relationships had deeper meaning than before. They didn't want to lose those moments that mattered. They didn't laugh much during their internment, but in America, they celebrated their freedoms through light-heartedness and jokes, usually at each other's expense. Their behavior was indicative of their appreciation for life, that everything in life is relative. "Make the best of your circumstances, and don't complain," was a recurring phrase in Hinck households. I adopted this attitude in my military career. Toward the beginning of my career as an Army aviator, I attended a survival school where I experienced the challenges associated with being a POW—surviving, evading, resisting, and escaping. Hearing of my schooling, my father quipped, "At seventy-four, after three years in a prison camp, a few days in a survival course would seem like summer camp." From that perspective, I understood everything in life is relative.

All of my deployments were challenging. In Albania, the water table was about a foot below the surface making foot and vehicle movement slow and difficult. In Iraq, the dust storms and heat posed constant challenges for Soldiers and aviators. In Afghanistan, the winters nearly caused a stoppage of action on all sides, and the high mountain altitudes made operations a task. Yet if my father could survive three years as a POW, then I could surely make it through a few months of war.

After a few deployments, whenever someone asked how I was doing, my normal response was, "I am doing great. Life could be worse, but I have food in my stomach, a warm place to sleep, a place to call home, and no one is shooting at me." I am thankful for my family's journey.

The Grit of My Grandmother, Dorothy Hinck, and the Hinck Bill

Just saying "grandmother" conjures images of a strong woman, wise in counsel and strong in soul. Add character, courage, persistence, and long, black hair atop a sturdy Chinese-Scottish woman who speaks five languages (Cantonese, Tagalog, English, Latin, and Spanish), throw in the tenacity of a bulldog, and you have my grandmother. As a young girl, Dorothy Allen Hinck grew up in Shanghai, China, and struggled with early childhood health problems. She moved to the Philippines to live with relatives for the better island climate.

She met and married John H. Hinck, my grandfather after whom I was named, who was serving in the U.S. Army on the islands. They had a great life raising their five kids. My grandfather rose through the enlisted ranks, became an officer, retired near Manila, and worked for the Port Authority.

When WWII arrived in the islands, life was tumultuous at best. Because of the war, my grandfather was recalled to active service but died in November 1941 from a heart attack on a Navy ship shortly after an invasion. My grandmother heard from the chaplain that her husband had died, and that the body was to be buried in a cemetery near Clark Air Force Base. There was no agency to assist with the funeral or provide a death certificate.

The Japanese invaded the islands in December 1941. My now-widowed grandmother and her five kids, including my father, were captured in early February 1942 and interned in prison camps. Their three-year internment in those harsh conditions ended with liberation in January 1945. The Philippines is the final resting place for over 60,000 Americans and almost 300,000 Japanese but estimates of the cost to Filipinos neared one million. The family was fortunate to survive and sought to renew their freedoms. My grandmother's courage and determination endured. I fast-forward to San Francisco, California, to the reception center where the Hincks landed. In my father's own words (as captured in the unpublished work, The Book of Ed: My Father's POW Story):

> *The immigration offices gave us a bad time. We were the last to get off of the boat. They questioned Mother's claim about being American. All of us children were on the list as being Americans, but Mother was English. Mom finally proved to the officials that she married Dad before the 1918 law was passed. Anyone who married an American in a foreign land became an American by taking his [the husband's] status as an American citizen. Immigration officials complained that mom was an illegal entering the States. But your grandmother finally convinced them that she was certainly an American citizen by showing them her marriage certificate.*
>
> *After immigration agents asked my grandmother to provide proof of citizenship in the form of her husband's death certificate, she replied with a stoic gaze: "As a POW for three years, where do you think I kept those kinds of papers?"*

My grandmother and her children were detained until the U.S. Army could find proper documentation and until other family on the east coast could vouch for them. My family relocated to Fresno in the center of the San Joaquin Valley of central California.

After establishing a new home there, my grandmother filed to claim her husband's benefits such as his pay and allowances, something to which surviving spouses of military members are entitled. Her initial request was denied. To receive the compensation, the claims division within the U.S. Department of Veterans Affairs needed proof she was legally married to John Hinck, certification of his service in the U.S. Army, and documentation that he had died in combat accompanied by a copy of his death certificate. Although she provided the faded marriage certificate and his Army service records, it took a while to get an actual copy of his death certificate.

After almost a year of waiting and working with several levels of government, she received an official death certificate. Her claim finally had all the proper documentation. However, the statute of limitations had expired. Again she was denied benefits. The wording of the law meant she had to claim benefits during her time as a POW, which clearly would have been impossible.

For the next three decades, my grandmother campaigned to change the law and amend the statute of limitations. She wrote more than twenty letters to government representatives, the Department of the Army, and Veterans Affairs seeking acceptance of her rightful claim to survivor benefits. With every denial, her determination and courage strengthened. Several elected officials, specifically Representative B.F. Sisk of California, and governmental agencies assisted in giving her cause a voice. Finally, after countless attempts spanning thirty-one years, on July 8, 1975, President Gerald Ford signed H.R. 2946, dubbed a "bill for the relief of Mrs. Dorothy Hinck":

> *Be it enacted by the Senate and House of Representatives of the United States of America in Congress assembled, That, notwithstanding the provisions of section 3010 of title 38, United States Code, or any statute of limitations, Mrs. Dorothy Hinck, widow of John Henry Hinck (XC-3,009,409) is to be held and considered to have filed a timely application for death*

compensation for herself and minor children within one year of the death of the said John Henry Hinck on November 24, 1941, and is to be paid the amounts due as otherwise provided in the laws administered by the Administrator of Veterans' Affairs. Approved July 8, 1975.

Subsequently, Private Law 94-14 was enacted, and future laws were amended to remove the requirement of a one-year statute of limitations. Future acceptance of claims was based on the merits of the claim. Over the thirty-one years she had fought for her rightful benefits, she also raised five children and headed the household so her children could have the opportunity for a better life. Despite the numerous challenges, my grandmother won her fight to change one of our nation's unjust laws. She could have given up any time amid the mounting periods of defeat. Yet my grandmother fought for what was right.

Grit is the combination of repeated persistence with unwavering courage. Today, the Hinck Bill stands as a testament to Dorothy Hinck's grit. Almost every successful person endures countless efforts with undaunted courage on a path to their own freedoms and success. It is grit that separates those who try and those who succeed. Life and grit are intertwined.

Letter to God

Dear God,

It's been a while since our last communion. I stopped talking with you, stopped going to church, and stopped believing in you years ago. Please forgive me. When I was eight and you took my brother, my dad said it was to a better place—the angels needed someone to make them smile. But when you let my mother suffer due to cancer and finally took her away in a hollowed shell, you caused my father enormous grief. My dad, a former POW, buried his own dad in WWII, as well as his young son and his true love years later. You asked more of my father than many I know. Who are you to ask so much of one person? Where was your compassion? Your love? Life is hard to understand. But I believe my own father, mother, and brother are making your angels smile right now. I believe they are in a better place. It's hard to forgive you.

I built my life for you and around you. And still you let me down. You called me to serve in your church as the youngest lay minister giving communion to the sick, and later as Parish Council President—in a church which trespassed upon the faithful and the innocent. The awful lies, the cover-ups, the sins committed. Where was your justice at the hearts of the misguided? You filled me with passion to serve my country, to do biddings in the name of freedom, and to make choices to end human life in the name of greater good yet made me hide in fear of retribution and humiliation, just for being gay. It's hard to forgive you.

You made me gay in a world which didn't accept me, in a church which denounced me, and with friends who shunned me. When I looked to your words and your spirit, they offered me little in the way of serving your faith in a gay way. I turned to other ways of being accepted and became an empty, lonely shell for a while. I made too many poor choices. I lost a love due to a lack of compassion and holding onto pain. I seek to forgive you, to forgive myself. It took some time, but I am feeling freer to be me. Now, it is not the issue of being gay that I grudge; I fully accept who I am in your eyes and sometimes the world's eyes. But the gospel lacks the space that covers faith, hope, and charity from, and for, my kind. How do I fit into your picture of life? Where is my place of service in a world worthy of your love and grace? How do I love my kind, all kind, as me through your eyes?

I am crossing the threshold of having the strength to find my own way and to make meaning of your love in a new way. You have given me a family that accepts me. You gave me a glimpse of great love. You brought me closer to my older brother. You brought my aunt into my life at time when I needed patience, grace, and gratitude. All those gifts have aided my journey and filled me with a true wisdom for life, a renewed patience in love, and a new way to love others. And I thank you for those blessings. But there is more for me to do and be. And more for me to become in your eyes, and in my own. Now help me see our path clearly and once again love more freely.

Love,
John

Thank You, Aunt Ethel

Forgiveness without gratitude kept me in the past and prevented being present with self and others. The summer before I began my Ph.D. program, my father and his sister (my aunt) were in a terrible automobile accident. My father was killed instantly, but my Aunt Ethel survived. Somewhat naively, I offered to my family that I could care for Aunt Ethel. Over the three years as her primary caregiver, my Aunt Ethel taught me many things of which gratitude and living in the moment were highlights. Living in the moment is about being present to self and others in the here and now.

Where *Chronos* is the linear concept of time, *Kairos* is more relational and alludes to what is happening in the moment. In elder care, time is relative, and the present moments are usually spent holding onto or remembering the past or avoiding the looming future.

Freud used the concept of *Ananke*, the Greek Goddess of Necessity, and *Eros*, the Greek God of Love, as parents of civilization. But in elder care, Ananke, in relation to time, can be considered what is needed or necessary in the moment. In elder care, Ananke is normally the choice of the caregiver as a response to the situation with the elder. The concept of "tough love" comes to mind when combining Eros and Ananke. For the caregiver, this alludes to what is needed in the moment for the physical and emotional health of the elder person, so Ananke takes precedence over Chronos or Kairos. But for the elder, it seems that living in the moment regardless may be more critical for health than dwelling on the past or avoiding the future; hence, Kairos becomes the driving force in relation to Chronos and Ananke. Due to the onset of dementia and less brain elasticity to remember, re-teaching forgotten skills was needed with my aunt. One day, we spent a few hours re-learning how to do small loads of laundry. Upon returning home from school later the same evening, I discovered that the tuxedo I had set out to wear at an event that night was not on the doorknob to the washing area. When I asked Aunt Ethel if she had moved my tux, she said, "Yes, I did." Upon further inquiry, she said with a very pleased look on her face, "I washed it for you, and it's in the dryer now."

My shock and dismay were held until I went into my room and screamed into a pillow. I came out of the room and hugged her and told her I was thankful for her thoughtfulness. How could I be truly mad at her when I had hung the clothes near the washing machine, she had proudly done what we had practiced earlier, and she was genuinely trying to help? The situation gave me the opportunity to wear my Army dress blues and to learn a lesson about forgiveness, live in the moment of her own joy, and with gratitude of a good laugh about the whole situation. Thank you, Aunt Ethel.

Our Leadership Apocalypse

At times, I am consumed with thoughts about how our world presents choices amid a series of cascading moments. We are leaders in the rye, the ryes of each other, ideally catching, holding, loving, and freeing. Yet our provenance and privilege limit us and strangle the hopes of many even as it secures their places. It feels like a leadership apocalypse. I want to have the attitude to feel positive about the outcomes. I want to have the aptitude of positivity of potential. I want to have an altitude of perspectives so that I can see the situation from the eyes of others. I want to do work that connects the head, heart, and hand.

The day my mother died, my father asked if my twin and I wanted to visit her. We had seen her so many times in that hospital room, fighting against the cancer which had increasingly spread throughout her body. The loss of hair, bed sores, and a host of other treatment that had produced further ailments had left a hollowed shell of what my mother once was—a vibrant, loving person and a gifted elementary teacher. I carried the guilt of not seeing her on that final day. I still dislike hospitals. A good friend once commented that I avoid getting too close in friendships in fear of losing the person. There could be some truth in the notion as I lost my older brother Stephen to Reye's syndrome when I was eight, and I lost my mother when I was thirteen. Fear is a powerful thing.

Thirty years later, that same notion may have affected my ten-year relationship with my first love. He was the first, and only long-term relationship. Like many relationships, we had some challenges. But instead of working to make things better, it was easier to walk away. A breakup is never just one person's fault, but I relied on pride for protection and harbored the pain and hurt which clouded any rationality of action.

My father died the summer before I started my Ph.D. program. He was killed in a car accident taking his older sister (my aunt) out for dinner. As he pulled out into the road, he didn't see the speeding car which hit his side of the vehicle. He was killed instantly, and my Aunt Ethel was severely injured. My dad had been having trouble seeing at night, and we had discussed ways to retain his driving freedom, like driving only during the daytime. I often think an earlier intervention could have prevented the accident. Part of the reason I decided to be the primary caregiver for my aunt stems from my feeling of partial responsibility regarding this incident.

Feeling guilty, the need for protection from loss and death, excessive self-pride, the harboring of pain, and acting responsible for past regrets or poor judgment all help to preserve oneself in some way. And those same mechanisms prevent the attainment of real love for oneself and for others, especially until forgiveness is enacted. My leadership apocalypse may be about forgiveness of self and abandoning resentment while fostering gratitude, empathy, and generosity. Forgiveness begins with first forgiving the person in the mirror.

In my book, *Strength and Honor,* I ended with a story called "The Running Father," where I used the story of the prodigal son from the Book of Luke and described how my father ran to others in accepting, believing, and supporting them. Looking back, I think I am my own father running to myself. We all are. And until we learn to forgive, to have gratitude in the present, and to act with courage to step into our future, then the leadership apocalypse will continue to lurk on the horizon for each of us, in our communities, and throughout the world.

The heart of a person is seen in seconds upon seconds of influences in life. The role of leaders is to develop others toward their potential and into a future that they may not yet see, but about which we must care. Leadership is about setting conditions for others to develop, which is at the heart of this book of diverse stories of leadership, character, and values. Our badges of honor increase belongingness, improve connections, and strengthen our social fabric. Because of this book, there are more leader-authors whose more than thirty-five stories will influence thousands toward a greater strength and honor for our world.

John's Leadership Lessons

1. Be thankful for your family's journey.

2. Journey and grit in life are intertwined.

3. Give gratitude freely and with intention.

4. Learn to gracefully forgive yourself and others.

5. Find the courage to grow into your own potential and empower others to do that same.

6. Discover your family's narrative of head-heart-hand stories that are full of strength and honor.

JOHN M. HINCK, PhD

John Hinck serves as the Assistant Professor of Leadership for the USAF's Leadership Institute, Air War College, and the Eaker Center for Leadership Development. With more than twenty-two years of serving as a combat leader, Colonel, and Apache Longbow pilot, John served with distinction in Korea, Germany, Bosnia, Albania, Iraq, and Afghanistan and commanded Army recruiting in the upper Midwest, the 3-214th Aviation Regiment, and TF ODIN-A in Afghanistan. After military service, John received his PhD in leadership studies from the University of San Diego and is a nationally board-certified coach specializing in executive leadership and leadership development. Through his teaching, research, consulting, and coaching, John has influenced thousands to make a difference in life and to lead and live with strength and honor.

My Leadership Stories

_____

Write your name above.

Please add your stories:

_____

_____

_____

_____

_____

_____

_____

_____

_____

_____

_____

_____

_____

_____

_____

_____

_____

_____